MODERN EUROPEAN PHILOSOPHY

Editors
ALAN MONTEFIORE, BALLIOL COLLEGE, OXFORD
HIDÉ ISHIGURO, UNIVERSITY COLLEGE LONDON

THE IDEA OF A CRITICAL THEORY
Habermas and the Frankfurt School

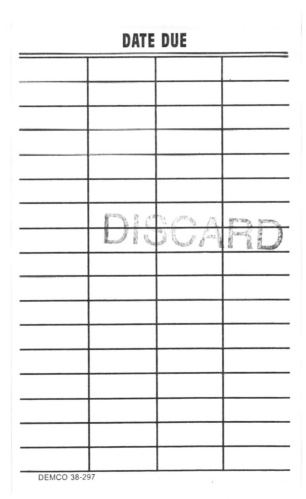

THE IDEA OF
A CRITICAL THEORY

Habermas and the Frankfurt School

RAYMOND GEUSS

CAMBRIDGE UNIVERSITY PRESS
CAMBRIDGE
LONDON   NEW YORK   NEW ROCHELLE
MELBOURNE   SYDNEY

Published by the Press Syndicate of the University of Cambridge
The Pitt Building, Trumpington Street, Cambridge CB2 1RP
32 East 57th Street, New York, NY 10022, USA
296 Beaconsfield Parade, Middle Park, Melbourne 3206, Australia

First published 1981

Printed in the United States of America

British Library Cataloguing in Publication Data
Geuss, Raymond
The idea of a critical theory. – (Modern
European philosophy)
1. Frankfurt School of Sociology
I. Title   II. Series
301'.01   M24   80-42274
ISBN 0 521 24072 7 hard covers
ISBN 0 521 28422 8 paperback

CONTENTS

		page
Editors' introduction		vii
Preface		x
List of abbreviations		xi
Introduction		
1	**Ideology**	4
	1 Ideology in the descriptive sense	4
	2 Ideology in the pejorative sense	12
	3 Ideology in the positive sense	22
	4 Ideologickritik	26
2	**Interests**	45
	1 Real interests	45
3	**Critical theory**	55
	1 Cognitive structure	55
	2 Confirmation	75
	3 Epistemology	88
Works cited		96
Index		98

EDITORS' INTRODUCTION

The purpose of this series is to help make contemporary European philosophy intelligible to a wider audience in the English-speaking world, and to suggest its interest and importance in particular to those trained in analytical philosophy.

Of course, as everyone knows, the labels 'analytical' and 'European' (or 'continental') are very unsatisfactory. Many of the philosophers who have influenced the recent tradition of analytical philosophy in important ways were born and bred on the European mainland, and, even if some moved later in their lives to the United States or to England, they first developed their thought in Europe and within the context of the European philosophical tradition. Some of them, indeed, may clearly be regarded both as 'continental' and as analytical philosophers in their own right. More generally, there has recently been a striking increase in the number of philosophers engaged in work of conceptual analysis on the continent of Europe. There is a long tradition of such work in Scandinavia and, for example, Poland; but it is now being more and more widely taken up in other countries, most notably perhaps in Germany.

Moreover, the universities of Europe which have been very little or not at all influenced by the analytical tradition – and these still include nearly all of those in France and Italy, and the great majority of those in German-speaking Europe and in Eastern Europe – have by no means represented any unitary tradition. The disagreements, amounting sometimes even to lack of any genuine communication, between, for instance, Hegelians, Marxists, phenomenologists and Thomists have often been deep. But these disagreements are still 'small' in comparison with the barriers of mutual ignorance and distrust which have persisted in recent times between the main representatives of the analytical tradition on the one hand and those of the main philosophical schools of the European continent on the other hand – schools which are also dominant in Latin America, Japan and even some universities in the USA and Canada. And these barriers are inevitably reinforced by the fact that, until very recently at any rate, even the best students from the universities situated on either side tend to emerge from their studies with such divergent areas of knowledge and ignorance, competence and incompetence, that they are hardly equipped even to enter into informed discussion with each other about the nature of what separates them.

The first book in this series was one by Charles Taylor on Hegel, and in introducing it we noted the appropriateness of such an inauguration; for, as we said, it is by reference to Hegel that one may indicate most starkly the difference between the two traditions to whose intercommunication the series seeks to contribute. This second book by Raymond Geuss submits to detailed conceptual scrutiny certain central theses of the Frankfurt School of philosophers and, in particular, of its most distinguished contemporary heir and successor, Jürgen Habermas. Habermas and the Frankfurt School stand explicitly in the line of development, reaction and counter-reaction to the philosophy of Hegel and to that of his successor – in so far as he is to be taken, controversially, as his successor – Marx. The Frankfurt School themselves certainly conceived of their own relationship to Marx in this light; and whatever one may think to be the best way to understand Marx' relation to Hegel, there can be no doubt of the importance and continuing influence of the School's reemphasis of what they took to be the Hegelian elements in Marx' thought. Their further elaborations of the characteristically Marxist notions of ideology and of false consciousness, and in particular Habermas' own notable attempt to articulate the contribution that 'critical philosophy' can make towards the development of a maximally enlightened self-awareness, lie at the heart of this influence; and it is these notions and this attempt that Raymond Geuss sets out to examine.

There is a further remark contained in that earlier introduction that bears particular relevance to the understanding of Habermas' work: 'The divergences that lie behind the development of these barriers can properly be understood only by reference back beyond Hegel to Kant, to the very different ways in which different schools of philosophy have reacted to his work and to the further counter-reactions of *their* successors.' For Habermas, as Geuss makes clear, is also to be considered as, in certain important ways, a transcendental philosopher.

Whether the use that Habermas makes of his transcendental heritage is an advantage or, as Raymond Geuss argues, a disadvantage is, no doubt, a properly debatable matter. But whatever the difficulties of principle there may perhaps be in the way of an at once genuinely dissentient and yet full understanding of the general Kantian tradition at any rate does not depend on acceptance of it. Indeed, the transformation of the divergent reactions to that tradition into veritable barriers is a relatively recent phenomenon. Brentano, writing on the philosophy of mind at the end of the last century, frequently referred to J. S. Mill and to other contemporary British philosophers. In turn, G. E. Moore refers to Brentano. Bergson discusses William James frequently in his works. For Husserl one of the most important philosophers was Hume. The thinkers discussed seriously by Russell include not only Frege and Poincaré, but also Meinong. How unfortunate, then, that those who have followed in their footsteps have refused to read or even to respect one another, the ones convinced that the others survive on undisciplined rhetoric and an irresponsible lack of rigour, the others suspecting the former of aridity, superficiality and over-subtle trivialisation.

But already, even in the short space of time since the writing of that earlier introduction, there have been further signs of a renewed respect for and willingness to listen to each other. Hopes should not – as yet, at any rate – be exaggerated. The distance and the differences remain for the moment at least as great as the points of rapprochement and of community of interest. Nevertheless, Habermas provides one excellent example of a major contemporary philosopher from the continent with a real interest in and knowledge of some of the most important central areas of analytic philosophy; and, as Raymond Geuss shows very well, his work provides readily accessible ground for stimulating and fruitful debate between philosophers of both traditions.

Geuss' book thus constitutes a very natural and appropriate member of this series, whose aim it is to present contributions by philosophers who have worked in the analytic tradition, but who now tackle problems specifically raised by philosophers of the main traditions to be found within contemporary Europe. They are works of philosophical argument and of substance rather than merely introductory résumés. We believe that they may contribute towards the continuing formation of a richer and less parochial framework of thinking, a wider frame within which mutual criticism and stimulation will be attempted and where mutual disagreements will at least not rest on ignorance, contempt or distortion.

PREFACE

To Robert Denoon Cumming I am indebted for over a decade of instruction and encouragement. I have profited particularly from discussions of the issues treated in the following pages with Richard Rorty and Quentin Skinner and from comments on the penultimate version of the manuscript by Hidé Ishiguro and Alan Montefiore. Many of the ideas in this book derive from Sidney Morgenbesser without whose constant help it wouldn't have come into being. It was a pleasure to work with Jeremy Mynott, Jonathan Sinclair-Wilson, and Francis Brooke (all of Cambridge University Press) on the preparation of the manuscript for publication. Finally special thanks to John Loesch.

ABBREVIATIONS

EI Habermas, Jürgen, *Erkenntnis und Interesse*, Frankfurt: Suhrkamp (second edition) 1973.

KK Habermas, Jürgen, *Kultur und Kritik*, Frankfurt: Suhrkamp, 1973.

LS Habermas, Jürgen, *Legitimationsprobleme im Spätkapitalismus*, Frankfurt: Suhrkamp, 1973.

N2 Habermas, Jürgen, 'Nachwort' to second edition of *Erkenntnis und Interesse*.

PP Habermas, Jürgen, *Philosophisch Politische Profile*, Frankfurt: Suhrkamp, 1971.

PS Adorno, Th. W. et al, *Der Positivismusstreit in der deutschen Soziologie*, Neuwied und Berlin: Luchterhand, 1969.

TG Habermas, Jürgen and Luhmann, Niklas, *Theorie der Gesellschaft oder Sozialtechnologie – Was leistet die Systemforschung?*, Frankfurt: Suhrkamp, 1971.

TP Habermas, Jürgen, *Theorie und Praxis*, Frankfurt: Suhrkamp (fourth edition) 1971.

TW Habermas, Jürgen, *Technik und Wissenschaft als 'Ideologie,'* Frankfurt: Suhrkamp, 1968.

WL Wellmer, Albrecht, *Kritische Gesellschaftstheorie und Positivismus*, Frankfurt: Suhrkamp, 1969.

WT Habermas, Jürgen, 'Wahrheitstheorien' in *Wirklichkeit und Reflexion: Festschrift für Walter Schulz*, Pfullingen: Neske, 1973.

ZL Habermas, Jürgen, *Zur Logik der Sozialwissenschaften*, Frankfurt: Suhrkamp, 1970

ZR Habermas, Jürgen, *Zur Rekonstruktion des historischen Materialismus*, Frankfurt: Suhrkamp, 1976.

English translations:

T 1 Habermas, Jürgen, *Knowledge and Human Interests*, translated by Jeremy Shapiro, Boston: Beacon Press, 1971.

T 2 Habermas, Jürgen, *Legitimation Crisis*, translated by Thomas McCarthy, Boston: Beacon Press, 1975.

T 3   Adorno, Th. W. et al., *The Positivist Dispute in German Sociology*, translated by Glyn Adey and David Frisby, New York: Harper, 1976.

T 4   Habermas, Jürgen, *Theory and Practice*, translated by John Viertel, Boston: Beacon Press, 1973.

T 5   Habermas, Jürgen, *Toward a Rational Society*, translated by Jeremy Shapiro, Boston: Beacon Press, 1970.

T 6   Wellmer, Albrecht, *Critical Theory of Society*, translated by John Cumming, New York: Seabury Press, 1971.

INTRODUCTION

This book deals with a claim made about the work of Marx. In outline this claim runs as follows:

It is widely recognized that Marx was a revolutionary figure, but the exact nature of the revolution he initiated has not, in general, been correctly understood. Of course, Marx did dramatically change many people's views about an important subject-matter, human society, but in some ways the greatest significance of his work lies in its implications for epistemology. Marx's theory of society, if properly construed, does clearly give us knowledge of society, but does not easily fit into any of the accepted categories of 'knowledge.' It obviously isn't a formal science like logic or mathematics, or a practical skill. Its supporters generally deny that it is a speculative world-view of the kind traditionally provided by religion and philosophy, yet neither would it seem to be correctly interpreted as a strictly empirical theory like those in natural science. Finally, it isn't just a confused mélange of cognitive and non-cognitive elements, an empirical economics fortuitously conjoined with a set of value judgments and moral commitments. Rather Marxism is a radically new kind of theory; to give a proper philosophic account of its salient features requires drastic revisions in traditional views about the nature of knowledge.

In what follows I will be concerned with a particular version of this claim propounded by a group of German philosophers known as the 'Frankfurt School.' I will use the term 'Frankfurt School' to include not only Horkheimer, Adorno, and the early Marcuse, but also such figures as Habermas and Wellmer. The members of the Frankfurt School think that Freud, too, was a conceptual revolutionary in more or less the sense in which Marx was, and that the theories of Marx and Freud exhibit such strong similarities in their essential epistemic structure that from a philosophical point of view they don't represent two different kinds of theory, but merely two instances of a single new type. The general name given to this new type of theory of which Marxism and psychoanalysis are the two main instances is 'critical theory.' The Frankfurt account of the essential distinguishing features of a 'critical theory' consists of three theses:

1. Critical theories have special standing as guides for human action in that:

(a) they are aimed at producing enlightenment in the agents who hold them, i.e. at enabling those agents to determine what their true interests are;

(b) they are inherently emancipatory, i.e. they free agents from a kind of coercion which is at least partly self-imposed, from self-frustration of conscious human action.

2. Critical theories have cognitive content, i.e. they are forms of knowledge.

3. Critical theories differ epistemologically in essential ways from theories in the natural sciences. Theories in natural science are 'objectifying'; critical theories are 'reflective.'

A critical theory, then, is a reflective theory which gives agents a kind of knowledge inherently productive of enlightenment and emancipation.

In Frankfurt usage a 'positivist' is a person who holds: (a) that an empiricist account of natural science is adequate, and (b) that all cognition must have essentially the same cognitive structure as natural science. If all theories in natural science have an 'objectifying' structure, then to assert that all cognition has the structure of natural science is to assert that all cognition is 'objectifying' cognition. So positivism can be seen as the 'denial of reflection,' i.e. as a denial that theories could be both reflective and cognitive.

Critical theories are particularly sensitive to the kind of philosophic error embodied in positivism. It is perfectly possible, the members of the Frankfurt School will claim, for persons with quite woefully mistaken epistemological views to produce, test, and use first-order theories in natural science, but this is not the case with critical theories. There is a close connection between having the right epistemology and ability to formulate, test, and apply first-order theories which successfully produce enlightenment and emancipation. For this reason positivism is no particular obstacle to the development of natural science, but is a serious threat to the main vehicles of human emancipation, critical theories. One basic goal of the Frankfurt School is the criticism of positivism and the rehabilitation of 'reflection' as a category of valid knowledge.

The main aim of this book, then, is to come to a clearer understanding of what a critical theory is supposed to be. In the interests of simplicity and concreteness I will focus on one purported instance of a critical theory, the 'critical theory of society' which supposedly arose from the work of Marx, and will restrict myself to only occasional passing references to psychoanalysis. The very heart of the critical theory of society is its criticism of ideology. Their ideology is what prevents the agents in the society from correctly perceiving their true situation and real interests; if they are to free themselves from social repression, the agents must rid themselves of ideological illusion. Can 'Ideologiekritik' form the basis of a critical theory as defined by the three theses?

I have tried to avoid as far as possible the question of whether the Frankfurt reading of Marx is or is not correct. To answer this question would require a full-scale analysis of Marx's work in more detail than I could give, and it isn't clear how the answer to this historical question would bear on my main concern, the possibility of a critical theory (in the sense defined by the three theses). I have decided to focus my discussion on the views of Habermas because his work is the most sustained attempt by a member of the Frankfurt School to get clear about the underlying epistemological assumptions of the critical theory, and so raises the issues that interest me in a particularly striking way.

Although it is not my intention to give a systematic exposition of the philosophical views of Habermas (much less of Adorno, Horkheimer, or Marcuse), I have tried to make my discussion as self-contained as possible and presuppose no acquaintance with his work.[1] The book sets itself the modest task of explaining clearly what a critical theory is supposed to be.

[1] The reader interested in the history of the Frankfurt School can profitably consult Jay (1973). Kortian (1980) is a good introduction to Habermas. I have been strongly influenced in my treatment of the Frankfurt School by the excellent Theunissen (1969).

1

⬦⬦⬦

IDEOLOGY

1 IDEOLOGY IN THE DESCRIPTIVE SENSE

The term 'ideology' is used in many different ways; this is at least partly due to the fact that social theorists have propounded theories of ideology in the course of trying to answer very different questions. I will try to distinguish three different research contexts within which theories of ideology have been developed; corresponding to each of these three research programs there will be a family of ways in which the term 'ideology' is used.[1]

The first of the three research programs I wish to distinguish is the program of an empirical study of human groups – call it 'anthropology.' There are various things one might wish to study about a given human group. One might study the biological and quasi-biological properties of the group – the birth-rate, the distribution of blood-type or human phenotype among the subgroups, the resistance to or incidence of various kinds of diseases, etc. Or one might wish to study the cultural or socio-cultural features of the group – the kinship system, pattern of land-tenure, artistic traditions, religious and scientific beliefs, legal institutions, values, agricultural technology, etc. Although this distinction between the biological properties of a group and its 'culture' or 'socio-cultural system' is rough and imprecise,[2] let us suppose that we know clearly enough what a 'culture' or a 'socio-cultural system' is that we can make it an object of empirical investigation. Thus, for any given human group we can undertake to describe the salient features of its socio-cultural system and how they change over time. If we have at our disposal descriptions of several human groups, we may begin to look for universal or invariant features which all cultures exhibit or for relations of concomitance among apparently distinct socio-cultural features; we

---

[1] Needless to say, the following discussion makes no claim to exhaust the various senses in which the term 'ideology' and its derivatives have been used. Vide Lichtheim (1967); Barth (1975); and Larrain (1979).

[2] Kroeber and Kluckhohn (1952) distinguish over a hundred senses of 'culture.' Vide also D. Kaplan and R. Manners (1972).

may try to elaborate a typology of human cultures, classifying them according to their similarities and differences; if we are bold, we may hazard hypotheses about why certain features are found in certain societies or why certain historical changes take place.

In the course of this kind of empirical inquiry we may subdivide the socio-cultural sphere into different 'parts' for further study. Thus, vulgar Marxists distinguish between (economic) base and (ideological) superstructure. Many twentieth-century anthropologists seem to prefer a tripartite scheme which distinguishes technology (or technology/economy), social structure, and ideology, and even more complicated schemes have been suggested.[3] A theory of ideology, then, can arise in the course of pursuing the project of describing and explaining certain features of or facts about human social groups; 'ideology' in the first sense will just refer to one of the 'parts' into which the socio-cultural system of a human group can be divided for convenient study. Depending on how the particular division is made, the 'ideology' of the group will be more or less extensive, but typically it will include such things as the beliefs the members of the group hold, the concepts they use, the attitudes and psychological dispositions they exhibit, their motives, desires, values, predilections, works of art, religious rituals, gestures, etc.[4] I will call 'ideology' in this very broad sense (including at least all of the above listed elements) 'ideology in the purely descriptive sense.' In this broad and rather unspecific sense of 'ideology' every human group has an ideology – the agents of any group will have some psychological dispositions, use some concepts, and have some beliefs. In particular 'ideology' in this sense does *not* comprise *only* those beliefs, habits, attitudes, traits, etc. *all* the members of a group share. Human groups contain variety, diversity, and conflict. The more detailed and complete we wish our account of a given group to be, the more it will have to contain descriptions of such differences of belief, motivation, preference, attitude, etc. Furthermore, this sense of 'ideology' is non-evaluative and 'non-judgmental'[5] – one isn't praising or blaming a group by asserting that its members 'have an ideology' in this sense.

An ideology in this merely descriptive sense will contain both discursive and non-discursive elements. By 'discursive' (or 'conceptual' or

---

[3] Sahlins distinguishes technology, social structure, and ideology (1968, pp. 14f). Service has: technology, economy, society, polity, and ideology (1966). Kaplan and Manners give: ideology, social structure, technoeconomics, personality (1972, p. 89). Probably there is no canonical division of the society into parts which would be applicable to all societies; in fact it is often claimed that a criterion of the 'primitiveness' of a society is the extent to which it lacks division between economy, society, kinship system, etc.

[4] Vide Kaplan and Manners (pp. 112f).

[5] Vide Kaplan and Manners (p. 113).

'propositional') elements I mean such things as concepts, ideas, beliefs, and by 'non-discursive' elements such things as characteristic gestures, rituals, attitudes, forms of artistic activity, etc.[6] This distinction between discursive and non-discursive elements is not the same as the distinction sometimes made (by Plamenatz, for instance) between explicit and implicit elements.[7] Clearly, discursive elements can be either explicit or implicit – agents can hold a particular belief explicitly or merely tacitly – but the distinction between 'explicit' and 'implicit' would seem to have no clear application to most non-discursive elements. It is hard to see what could be meant by calling a particular melody or gesture 'implicit' or 'explicit' in the sense under consideration here. Nevertheless, I would like to leave open the possibility of distinguishing between explicit and implicit non-discursive elements at least in *some* cases. It doesn't seem so odd to speak of attitudes, for instance, as being explicit or implicit.[8]

Finally neither of the two distinctions made above is identical with Plamenatz's distinction between unsophisticated and sophisticated elements of an ideology.[9] A belief can be quite explicit but unsophisticated, as can a taste or preference.

Since I don't want to try to give definitions of the terms used in these distinctions, perhaps an examination of an example will clarify their use. If one examines the religion of a group, one might discover that the performance of a particular ritual plays an important role – one might think here, for instance, of the role Baptism or the Eucharist play in Christianity. Of course, if the ritual is particularly important, it is unlikely that the agents who perform it will lack a term for it, but still a ritual is a set of actions, of things done, not itself a concept or belief.[10]

---

[6] On p. 345 of ZR Habermas speaks of 'die nichtpropositionalen Zeichensysteme der Literatur, der Kunst, und der Musik.' This is another one of those distinctions which are easier to see than to formulate exactly. One might want to claim that *all* the elements of an ideology are symbolically organised – certainly paintings, pieces of music, dances etc. are highly organised, but the organisation is not conceptual; a piece of music may have a meaning, even if one wishes to speak this way (I don't particularly) a 'grammar,' but that meaning is not a proposition. Naturally, too, by 'beliefs' I don't mean just simple empirical beliefs, but also normative beliefs, metaphysical beliefs etc.

[7] Plamenatz, pp. 17f, 21ff.

[8] Tastes, preferences, and predilections, too, can be either explicit or implicit. Certain of my tastes and preferences may simply express themselves in my customary mode of behavior. I may show no tendency to make much of them; I may in fact not even realize that I have them. We may wish to contrast this kind of case in which my tastes and preferences are 'merely implicit' with other cases in which I recognize, articulate, and cultivate a particular taste or preference. That in this second case I may be able to glory in my predilections only if I have certain beliefs, does not imply that the predilections, tastes, or preferences themselves *are* beliefs.

[9] Plamenatz, pp. 18ff.

[10] Vide Burkert, esp. chapter 11.

The religion is part of the ideology of the group; the ritual is a non-discursive element of the ideology. Given that rituals can have a long life – baptism and eucharist in some recognizable form have been around for at least a couple of millennia, and, even if one takes stricter criteria of identity, the particular form of the rituals defined for the Catholic Church by the Council of Trent standardized a practice that remained more or less unchanged for half a millennium – it is likely that at different historical periods the ritual will have been associated with quite different sets of implicit beliefs and attitudes. Peasants in the Abruzzi in 1600 and English Catholics in Toronto in 1950 both participated in the 'same' ritual of baptism, but, given the enormous other differences between these two groups, it would be amazing if the members of the two groups had the same implicit attitudes toward the ritual, beliefs about it, etc. Again what sorts of beliefs and attitudes most people in the society naively associate with the ritual, or 'express' by participating in it, may be very different from the conflicting theological interpretations conceptually sophisticated members of the society give to the ritual. So at one extreme one has a set of ritual actions, a 'non-discursive element' in the ideology, and at the other a perhaps very sophisticated, explicit theology – a body of systematically interconnected propositions – and in between varying kinds of more or less explicit and more or less sophisticated beliefs, attitudes, habits, etc.

For certain purposes it may be useful or desirable to single out for further study certain subsets of the set of all the beliefs, attitudes, concepts, etc. a group of agents has or uses. Since there doesn't seem to be any uniquely legitimate way to subdivide what I have called the 'ideology in a purely descriptive sense,' there will be a plurality of such divisions, and, corresponding to each distinguished part, a narrower, but perfectly legitimate descriptive sense of 'ideology.'[11] Thus, I may decide that I would like to retain a close connection between 'ideology' and 'idea,' and hence use the term 'ideology' to refer only to the beliefs of the agents in the society, i.e. only to the 'discursive elements' of the ideology (in the purely descriptive sense).

Habermas, in strong contrast to the earlier members of the Frankfurt School, does seem to use the term 'ideology' to refer in the first instance to the beliefs the agents in a society hold. The obvious next step, then, is to try to divide the set of all the beliefs the agents in the society hold into more or less 'natural' parts. One might then start to use the term 'ideology' yet more narrowly to refer to some subset of the set of all the

[11] Of course, certain divisions may be more useful or illuminating than others. My general 'purely descriptive sense' of ideology corresponds roughly to Mannheim's 'total sense' (cf. Mannheim, pp. 54ff); my 'narrower version' of ideology to his 'special sense' (p. 77).

discursive elements. Habermas' discussion of ideology suggests that he countenances two major ways of subdividing the set of all the agents' beliefs, and hence of distinguishing between kinds of ideologies in the very narrow sense: (1) One can distinguish between 'ideologies' (i.e. subsets of the set of all beliefs) on the basis of differences in their 'manifest content,'[12] i.e. by reference to differences in what the beliefs are beliefs *about*. So a set of beliefs about superhuman entities who are thought to supervise and enforce standards of human behavior may be called a 'religious ideology,' while a set of concepts for talking about economic transactions is an 'economic ideology.' (2) One can distinguish between ideologies in this very narrow sense in terms of their functional properties. By 'functional properties' I mean the way the elements of the ideology influence action.[13] So in this sense a set of beliefs of no matter *what* manifest content which significantly influences economic behavior could be called an 'economic ideology,' a set of beliefs and attitudes which significantly influences religious practices a 'religious ideology.'

In many cases there will be a close connection between the two senses of 'ideology' – or at least between concrete ideologies in the two senses. Thus a 'religious ideology' can be either a set of beliefs ostensibly about superhuman entities, i.e. a set of beliefs with a religious 'manifest content' or a set of beliefs and attitudes which in fact function to regulate or otherwise influence religious behavior or practices. There is the obvious difficulty with this second sense of 'ideology' that there isn't any such thing as 'specifically religious behavior' (except perhaps for some ritual behavior) or 'purely economic behavior' or what have you; actions and institutions don't come neatly boxed into well-defined and easily identifiable types. Often one may not know how to classify a particular bit of behavior or an institution – is it a religious ceremony, an economic institution, a political institution, or some combination of all three? Furthermore there may be differences between the classification the participating agents would prefer to give and the classification we, as outside observers, might prefer. Even if there aren't difficulties in principle about the basic classification of a certain bit of behavior as a 'religious ritual', it may also have political or economic aspects, overtones, or implications. The more indeterminate the notion of 'religious behavior' is

[12] TW 160 [T1 311]. Habermas speaks of 'der manifeste Gehalt von Aussagen.' Some of the essays in TW are translated in T 5, but the one cited here is translated as an appendix to T1.

[13] Non-discursive elements cannot be 'about' anything in the way in which propositions can, but they can have functional properties, so the 'religious ideology' in this functional sense might well be taken to include pictures, chants, etc.

allowed to become, the less well-defined will be the beliefs which might influence such behavior.

But despite the generally close connection between ideologies in the two senses, it is important to retain the distinction because some of the most interesting cases will be ones in which there are significant differences between the manifest content of the beliefs in an ideology and their functional properties – a set of 'religious and philosophical' beliefs about the nature of the gods may actually serve to regulate economic and political transactions. It will in general be an important fact about a given society how the various kinds of acts and institutions are individuated, how large a class of acts are considered to be 'purely economic transactions' or acts to which religious beliefs are directly relevant,[14] in other words, what kinds of beliefs, beliefs of what kind of manifest content, will be able to function as ideologies for what domains of action.

In these senses, then, the group may have more than one ideology – it may have a religious ideology *and* an economic ideology, and the two may not appreciably overlap. 'Ideologies' in these narrower senses are different from 'Ideology in a purely descriptive sense' in an important way: Every human group is composed of members who have *some* beliefs, and so every human group has an 'ideology in the descriptive sense,' but not every group will have an ideology in each of the possible narrower senses – since hunting-and-gathering bands have no state, and, *a fortiori*, no state-finances, they won't have a 'fiscal ideology' either.

In addition to speaking of 'the political ideology' of the group or 'the ideology for economic behavior' social theorists and others often speak of '*the*' ideology of the group simpliciter. Sometimes 'the' ideology of the group seems to mean nothing more than:

(a) the set of all those concepts and beliefs which do *not* contribute to production 'in virtue of the material character of production'[15]
(b) the set of all the moral and normative beliefs[16]
(c) the set of beliefs the agents have about themselves as social agents.[17]

But often 'the' ideology of a group seems to mean the world-view or 'world-picture' of the group. This notion of ideology as world-view is *not* identical with our original 'ideology in a purely descriptive sense.' The 'ideology of a group in the purely descriptive sense' comprises *all*

---

[14] Geertz (1971), gives examples of the way in which the sphere of what is identified as 'religious behavior' can vary even within the 'same' religious tradition.
[15] Cohen, pp. 47; 33f, 45–7, 88ff. McMurtry, pp. 125f, 128, 130ff, 140.
[16] Plamenatz, pp. 323ff. For a related use vide Barry, p. 39.
[17] In the *Deutsche Ideologie* Marx speaks of ideology as the agents' 'Illusionen und Gedanken über sich selbst,' Marx, vol. 3, pp. 46f; 13.

the beliefs members of the group hold (or perhaps – if this notion seem too all-encompassing and too indiscriminate to be of any use at all – it includes the characteristic beliefs widely shared among the members of the group), but of course not all the beliefs the members of a group hold belong to their world-view. Even beliefs which are widely shared and quite distinctive of members of the group need not belong to the world-view in the most normal sense of 'world-view.'

The intuition which motivates the introduction of a concept of 'ideology as world-view' is that individuals and groups don't just 'have' randomly collected bundles of beliefs, attitudes, life-goals, forms of artistic activity, etc. The bundles generally have some coherency – although it is very hard to say in general in what this coherency consists – the elements in the bundle are complexly related to each other, they all somehow 'fit,' and the whole bundle has a characteristic structure which is often discernible even to an outside observer. By an 'ideology in the sense of "world-view" ' then is meant a subset of the beliefs which constitute the ideology of the group (in a purely descriptive sense) which has the following properties:

(a) the elements in the subset are widely shared among the agents in the group
(b) the elements in this subset are systematically interconnected
(c) they are 'central to the agents' conceptual scheme' in Quine's sense, i.e. the agents won't easily give them up[18]
(d) the elements in the subset have a wide and deep influence on the agents' behavior or on some particularly important or central sphere of action
(e) the beliefs in the subset are 'central' in that they deal with central issues of human life (i.e. they give interpretations of such things as death, the need to work, sexuality, etc.) or central metaphysical issues.[19]

These properties are no more than very loosely defined, and whether or not any purported 'world-view' has any one of them is a question of degree – just how wide an influence on the agents' actual behavior must a set of elements have in order to qualify as part of the world-view of those agents? Also there is no canonical principle of ordering or weighting the various properties. So even if there were to be agreement that these five properties specify what we mean by the 'world-view' of a group, there would still be much room for disagreement in particular

[18] W. V. O. Quine, 1963, pp. 42ff.
[19] At KK 391 Habermas calls 'world-pictures' 'Interpretationen der Welt, der Natur, und der Geschichte im Ganzen.'

cases about what should count as 'the' world-view or 'the' ideology of this particular group. Whether or not every human group will have a world-view (in the way that every group has an ideology in the purely descriptive sense) will depend partly on how strictly one construes the five properties, but also partly on how one decides to pick out human groups. Up to now we have tacitly allowed groups to be picked out any way at all. Of course it would not be correct to assume that any group of agents individuated by some biological, ethnic, economic, social, political, or linguistic criterion will share the same, one world-view. This, of course, is quite a strong (and quite an implausible) empirical assumption.

The last descriptive sense of 'ideology' I would like to consider is what I will call 'ideology in the programmatic sense.' This sense is related to the sense in which the term 'ideology' is used by Daniel Bell and other proponents of the 'end of ideology' thesis. Bell calls an ideology 'a way of translating ideas into action'[20] and defines a 'total ideology' as an 'all-inclusive system of comprehensive reality, it is a set of beliefs, infused with passion, and seeks to transform the whole of a way of life.'[21] So a 'total ideology' is

(a) a program or plan of action[22]
(b) based on an explicit, systematic model or theory of how the society works
(c) aimed at radical transformation or reconstruction of the society as a whole
(d) held with more confidence ('passion') than the evidence for the theory or model warrants.[23]

The addition of '(d)' makes this no longer a descriptive or non-judgmental use of the term 'ideology' but rather a pejorative use. Even without '(d)' however, the definition is still rather tendentious in that the presence of '(c)' makes it artificially easy for Bell-style liberals to deny that they have an 'ideology' (because, presumably, liberals are not

---

[20] Bell in Waxman, p. 88.
[21] Bell in Waxman, p. 96. Bell is not very careful in attributing this notion to Mannheim. This is not the definition Mannheim gives of 'total ideology' when he introduces it in *Ideology and Utopia* (pp. 55f.); there is no implication that a 'total ideology' (for Mannheim) is a program of action for the transformation of a whole way of life.
[22] Vide Friedrich and Brzezinski, p. 75: 'Ideologies are essentially action-related systems of ideas. They typically contain a program and a strategy for its realization.'
[23] I may be reading more into the phrase 'infused with passion' than is intended. I'm obviously trying to assimilate Bell's view here with that of e.g. Popper, who seems to think that a theory of the society as a whole can have so little evidentiary support that *any* degree of confidence in it as a guide to radical transformation of society is more than is warranted. Vide Popper, 1971, ch. 9; Popper, 1964, sections 21ff.

at present in the US and the Western European countries in favor of 'radical transformation of society as a whole'). I will call '(a)' and '(b)' of Bell's 'total ideology' (*without* '(c)' and '(d)' as *necessary* components) an 'ideology in the programmatic sense.'[24]

2 IDEOLOGY IN THE PEJORATIVE SENSE

The second research program within which a theory of ideology may arise is a program of criticism of the beliefs, attitudes, and wants of the agents in a particular society. This research program is initiated by the observation that agents in the society are deluded about themselves, their position, their society, or their interests. The aim of the project is to demonstrate to them *that* they are so deluded. It might turn out that one can only convince them that they are deluded if one can explain to them *why* they hold the beliefs and attitudes they do, or one might have an independent theoretical interest in understanding and explaining how it came about that the agents developed this delusion, and why they continue to suffer from it – the theoretical interest will be all the greater, the more the delusion seems to have the result that the agents act contrary to what is manifestly in their own true interest. Still, in essence this is *not* an explanatory project like the first research program in section 1. Rather the point is to free the agents from a particular kind of delusion. In most of the interesting cases the ideological delusion to be rooted out (it is claimed) is not an empirical error even of a very sophisticated kind, but something quite different.

The basic use of the term 'ideology' in this program is a negative, pejorative, or critical one. 'Ideology' is '(ideological) delusion' or '(ideologically) false consciousness.'[25] I will use the term 'form of consciousness' to refer to a particular constellation of beliefs, attitudes, dispositions, etc.[26] So the basic question posed in this research program is: In

---

[24] Clearly if 'ideology' means 'ideology in the programmatic sense' liberals do have an ideology – they have a general view of society and how it works, and, more important, a general view about how it ought to work. Part of that general view is that certain kinds of decisions should be decentralized. This might seem to make the notion of a programmatic ideology vacuous: that is, the 'program for action' may be the 'action' of *not* interfering with certain parts of the economy and society. Still it seems to me not just a quibble to distinguish between cases like those of perhaps certain hunting-and-gathering societies in which people just don't make and implement certain kinds of plans for social action at all, and cases in which people espouse laissez-faire as a doctrine, and act on the theory that society is best run when certain possible kinds of centralized planning are avoided.

[25] WL 73, 95, 104 [T6 71, 90, 99], TP 435ff.

[26] LS 48 [T2]. So a 'form of consciousness' is an ideology in one of the narrower descriptive senses, i.e. a particular systematically interconnected subset of the set of all the beliefs, attitudes, etc. the agents of a group hold. I will henceforth use this term 'form of consciousness' because I would like to reserve 'ideology' to mean 'ideology in the pejorative

what sense or in virtue of what properties can a form of consciousness be ideologically false, i.e. can it be an ideology in the pejorative sense? I will consider three kinds of answers to this question:

(a) a form of consciousness is ideologically false in virtue of some *epistemic* properties of the beliefs which are its constituents;
(b) a form of consciousness is ideologically false in virtue of its *functional* properties;
(c) a form of consciousness is ideologically false in virtue of some of its *genetic* properties.

In the next few pages I will try to explain what I mean by each of these three ways of answering the question: What makes a form of consciousness an ideology?

I. By the 'epistemic properties' of a form of consciousness I mean such things as whether or not the descriptive beliefs contained in the form of consciousness are supported by the available empirical evidence, or whether or not the form of consciousness is one in which beliefs of different epistemic type (e.g. descriptive beliefs and normative beliefs) are confused. I will now consider four ways of using the term 'ideology'; in each case a form of consciousness will be considered to be ideological in virtue of some epistemic properties.

1. A form of consciousness is an ideology if it is essentially dependent on mistaking the epistemic status of some of its apparently constituent beliefs. As an example of what I mean by 'mistaking the epistemic status of a belief' consider the early positivist view that a proposition has cognitive content or is cognitively meaningful if and only if it is empirically verifiable, that is, if and only if it has some kind of observational content. To take a belief which is *not* empirically verifiable as being cognitively meaningful is to make a mistake about its epistemic status. Thus, on this view, all theological forms of consciousness are to be rejected as ideological because a theological form of consciousness is presumably a structured set of beliefs, attitudes, etc. which depends essentially on the assumption that there can be cognitively significant discourse about gods. Since beliefs about gods are not empirically verifiable – they don't have cognitive content – a theological form of consciousness is based on a mistake about the epistemic standing of one of its central constitutive beliefs. Note that to say that all *theological* forms of consciousness

sense' i.e. *'false* consciousness.' So from now on, 'ideology' unless further specified means 'ideology in the pejorative sense.' Also KK 334, TP 310 [T4 257], EI 16 [T1 8], WL 96, 105 [T6 90f, 100]. [Note that in this last passage 'Bewußtseinsformationen' ('forms of consciousness') is mistranslated as 'information of consciousness.']

are 'ideology' for the positivist is not to say that all forms of religious belief are 'ideology' (in the pejorative sense); the positivist can have no objection to religious beliefs as long as they don't pretend to be forms of knowledge.

This usage of 'ideology' is not dependent on accepting the verification theory of meaning. I might well reject the verification theory of meaning and still, for instance, think that value judgments had very different conditions of verification from descriptive beliefs, and hence a very different 'epistemic standing.' I might then want to call forms of consciousness 'ideological' if they presented value judgments as statements of fact.[27]

2. A form of consciousness is ideological if it contains essentially an 'objectification' mistake, i.e. if it contains a false belief to the effect that some social phenomenon is a natural phenomenon, or, to put it another way, human agents or 'subjects' are suffering from ideologically false consciousness if they falsely 'objectify' their own activity, i.e. if they are deceived into taking that activity to be something 'foreign' to them,[28] especially if they take that activity to be a natural process outside their control.

3. A form of consciousness is ideologically false if it contains a false belief to the effect that the particular interest of some subgroup is the general interest of the group as a whole.[29]

4. A form of consciousness is ideologically false if it mistakes self-validating or self-fulfilling beliefs for beliefs which are not self-validating or self-fulfilling. The notion of a 'self-validating or self-fulfilling belief' is modelled on Merton's notion of a 'self-fulfilling prophecy.'[30] If we think members of a subgroup G are lazy, unreliable, and unintelligent, and hence act toward them in ways which make them become lazy, unreliable, and unintelligent, the belief that the members of G are lazy etc. is self-fulfilling. There is nothing *inherently* wrong with holding self-fulfilling beliefs, as long as one *knows* that they are self-fulfilling. What is objectionable is the *use* of self-fulfilling beliefs in a context of justification of action where their justificatory force depends

---

[27] Gustave Bergmann uses 'ideology' in this sense: 'a value judgment disguised as or mistaken for a statement of fact I shall call an "ideological statement" ' (Brodbeck, p. 129).

[28] N2 400f and TG 246 where Habermas claims that Marx develops the notion of ideology 'als Gegenbegriff zu einer Reflexion ... durch die falsches Bewußtsein, nämlich die notwendigen Täuschungen eines Subjekts über seine eigenen, ihm fremd gewordenen Objektivationen zerstört werden kann.' The classic Marx passage is the chapter on the fetishism of commodity production in the first volume of *Kapital*, Marx, vol. 23, pp. 85ff.

[29] TG 289; KK 336, 391; and the discussion in Part III of LS. Standard loci from Marx are vol. 3, pp. 359ff, 374ff.

[30] Merton, pp. 421ff.

on misconstruing them as non-self-fulfilling, i.e. depends on mistaking their epistemic standing.[31]

II. The second kind of answer to the question, What makes a form of consciousness an ideology?, was: A form of consciousness is an ideology in virtue of some of its functional properties. I will consider three specific versions of this functional approach.

1. A form of consciousness is an ideology in virtue of the function or role it plays in supporting, stabilizing, or legitimizing certain kinds of social institutions or practices. Habermas regularly speaks of an ideology as a 'world-picture' which stabilizes or legitimizes domination or hegemony (Herrschaft).[32] It is in virtue of the fact that it supports or justifies reprehensible social institutions, unjust social practices, relations of exploitation, hegemony, or domination that a form of consciousness is an ideology.

Habermas

But, of course, the above isn't yet an unambiguous view. One must distinguish between the function of supporting, fostering, or stabilizing hegemony and the function of justifying or legitimizing hegemony. Any set of beliefs which legitimizes or justifies a social practice will thereby tend to support it, but the converse is not the case: a belief that a given ruling class is strong and ruthless, so that any resistance to the dominant social order is futile, may well be a belief, the acceptance of which by large segments of the population will have the effect of stabilizing the existing relations of dominance, but it is unlikely that such a belief could be used to *justify* these relations.[33] So 'herrschaftsstabilisierendes Bewußtsein' is not identical with 'herrschaftslegitimierendes Bewußtsein.'

Note further that neither of these two kinds of 'consciousness' is identical with the kind of consciousness intended in the famous slogan definition of ideology as 'socially necessary illusion.' The statement 'Form of consciousness f "stabilizes" hegemony' can be interpreted in two different ways: (a) 'Form of consciousness f contributes to the stability of hegemony (but it is an open question whether or not this contribution is sufficient to insure that the hegemony remains intact)' – 'stabilize' is used here as an 'attempt-verb.' (b) 'Form of consciousness f is successful in causing the hegemony to remain intact' – 'stabilize' is used here as a

---

[31] Note that most self-fulfilling beliefs are beliefs which embody an objectification mistake.

[32] An ideology for Haberman is 'herrschaftslegitimierendes Weltbild' or a 'herrschaftsstabilisierendes Weltbild.' TG 120f, 239ff, 246f, 258; TW 72 [T5 99]; LS 34 [T2 19]; etc. ZR 53; TG 257ff, 279, 289.

[33] Although it might be used by an individual to justify some action e.g. refusal to join an abortive uprising.

'success-verb.' So at best (namely, if 'stabilize' is interpreted as a 'success-verb') 'Form of consciousness f stabilizes hegemony' means that form of consciousness f is a *sufficient* condition for the continued existence of given relations of dominance, not that it is *necessary* for the functioning or reproduction of the society. Similarly, the fact that some beliefs in a form of consciousness are used to legitimate some social practice or institution in no way implies that those beliefs are the *only* ones which could be used, much less that the practice in question would cease to exist if they could no longer be used to legitimize it.

We also require further clarification of the notion of 'Herrschaft.' I will distinguish several 'semantic components' in the notion of 'Herrschaft.'[34]

A. 'Herrschaft' means the power to repress, i.e. to enforce frustration of some given human preferences. But this is clearly not an adequate or sufficient characterization of 'Herrschaft.' What is at issue here is the *critical* use of the term 'ideology.' But that means that to show that something is an ideology should be to show that we ought somehow to try to eliminate it. It seems unrealistic under the present conditions of human life to assume that any and every preference human agents might have can be satisfied, or to assume that all conflict between the preferences of different agents will be peacefully and rationally resolved. *Some* frustration – even some imposed frustration – of *some* human preferences must be legitimate and unexceptionable. But then to show that a form of consciousness is an ideology in the sense that it functions to support 'Herrschaft' is not yet to give any reason at all to eliminate it.

B. 'Herrschaft' is the exercise of power within a political order and is linked with some kind of *claim* to legitimacy. If a group of invaders simply ransacks a country, doing and taking what they want by sheer force, they will clearly be frustrating the preferences of the agents on whom they act, but they are not exercising 'Herrschaft' in the sense intended here. 'Normative repression' is frustration of agents' preferences which makes a claim to legitimacy that is accepted by those agents because of certain normative beliefs they hold.[35] 'Herrschaft' is power to exercise normative repression. This, too, is not yet an adequate account of 'Herrschaft' for the obvious reasons: There is nothing wrong with 'supporting or legitimizing Herrschaft' if the claim the 'Herrschaft' makes to legitimacy is valid.

C. 'Herrschaft' is normally unequally distributed; it is the domination

---

[34] The following discussion is based primarily on TG 246f, 254, 285ff, ZR 336.
[35] TG 254.

of one group *over* another. So, in general, a society in which 'Herrschaft' is exercised will be one in which some groups have a much higher level of frustration of their preferences than others do. The society may be extraordinarily repressive, as many egalitarian communities are, but, as long as the power to repress is equally distributed, it would be odd to speak of 'Herrschaft' being exercised.

But this concept of 'Herrschaft' is not adequate for use in our account of ideology, either. Unless unequal distribution of the power to exercise normative repression were *always* illegitimate, showing that a form of consciousness supported or legitimized this distribution of power would in no way imply that the form of consciousness was to be rejected. Marxists at least don't think that questions of the 'legitimacy' of social institutions can be answered 'abstractly,' that is, apart from consideration of the actual historical situation in which such questions arise. Marxists are also committed to the view that at certain levels of development of the material forces of production an unequal distribution of repressive normative power is historically necessary, i.e. necessary for the society to maintain and reproduce itself. If a certain distribution of power is 'necessary' there seems no point in questioning its legitimacy.

We probably *would* like to call unequal distribution of power to exercise normative repression 'Herrschaft.' Feudal lords *do* exercise 'Herrschaft' over their serfs, even if such 'Herrschaft' is historically necessary (at some particular moment in history). Showing that a form of consciousness supports unequal distribution of power does not in itself give us reason to reject the form of consciousness – unless we *also* know that this distribution of power is not at present necessary.

D. To say that a society imposes 'surplus repression' on its members is to say that it frustrates their preferences to a greater extent than is necessary for it to maintain and reproduce itself.[36] So 'surplus repression' refers to the total amount of aggregate repression in the society without reference to how this repression is distributed among the members. If 'Herrschaft' is defined as above in C, let 'surplus Herrschaft' mean more 'Herrschaft' than is needed for the society to maintain and

---

[36] This is Habermas' sense of 'surplus repression' (vide EI 80 [T1 57f], TG 290) which is probably not the same as Marcuse's, p. 32, where 'surplus repression' means 'restrictions required by social domination.' If 'social domination' means 'unequal distribution of normative power,' then there can be repression 'required by social domination' which is *not* 'surplus' in Habermas' sense. Thus in a 'hydraulic' society, the priests as a class may have more normative power than the peasants, and the priests may typically impose a certain amount of repression on the peasants in order to insure their continued domination – this repression is 'surplus' on Marcuse's view. *If* this drastically unequal distribution of normative power is the only way in which a society which has a very low level of productivity and depends on large-scale irrigation can function and reproduce itself, the 'repression' extracted by the priests to maintain their position is not 'surplus' in Habermas' sense.

reproduce itself.[37] We could then define 'ideology' as 'a form of consciousness which supports or legitimizes surplus Herrschaft.' But why should we reject a form of consciousness if we discover that it supports or legitimizes surplus Herrschaft? Is surplus Herrschaft always illegitimate? Why?[38]

2. The second kind of functional definition takes 'ideology' to be any form of consciousness which hinders or obstructs the maximal development of the forces of material production. This view is usually associated with a reading of Marx which takes him as positing the development of the forces of material production as an inherent goal of human societies.[39] It isn't hard to see a connection between this notion and 'surplus repression' – if a form of consciousness hinders the development of the forces of production it will obviously impose on the agents in the society more repression than they need suffer – but any connection with surplus Herrschaft is harder to see. Perhaps one could make an argument from the plausible motivation of agents – no agents in the society would have a motivation to impose more repression than necessary unless the surplus repression differentially benefited some group in the society more than others. Then the members of the privileged group would have such a motivation.

3. Finally we might call a form of consciousness which served to 'mask social contradictions'[40] an 'ideology.' Since 'masking social contradictions' might include such things as diverting attention from them, a form of consciousness might successfully mask social contradictions without containing any false beliefs. The concept of a 'social contradiction' is too complex and obscure to be adequately treated here. Note however, that if we take the 'major' contradiction in a social formation to be the contradiction between the relations of production and the forces of production, and if we take this 'contradiction' to consist in the fact that the relations of production fetter the development of the forces, it is not difficult to see how one might move from this third functional approach to ideology to the second.[41]

[37] In most normal cases, where there is surplus repression, there will also be surplus 'Herrschaft,' for what could motivate agents collectively to impose upon themselves more repression than is needed, unless the 'fruits' of that surplus repression are distributed unequally? In that case the beneficiaries of the unequal distribution will have a stake in its continuance.

[38] The question is whether 'illegitimate repression' is a separate category. Might there not be Herrschaft, surplus repression, etc. which is not illegitimate? Might there not also be kinds of illegitimate repression which are not either surplus or instances of Herrschaft? This question will become important in Chapter 3.

[39] Vide Cohen (1978). The members of the Frankfurt School recognize this strand in Marx, but think it is a mistake, WL 73 [T6 70f].

[40] Larrain, pp. 45ff.

[41] Vide Cohen, chs. VI, X, XI.

Ideology in the pejorative or critical sense was to be some kind of delusion or *false* consciousness. Granted that an ideology in one or another of the above 'functional' senses would be something eminently worthy of being rejected by the members of any known human society, would such an ideology be rejected *because* it is a delusion or because it is in some sense *false*? A form of consciousness may contain all kinds of non-discursive elements; it isn't clear how such elements *could* be false. Even the beliefs in a form of consciousness might be worthy of being rejected or given up on all kinds of grounds other than that they are delusions – they may be obnoxious, insensitive, immoral, nasty, ugly, etc. If I know that a form of consciousness I hold contributes to more massive frustration of my own preferences than necessary I may feel that I have grounds to give it up or change it, but does that mean that I think it is 'false' or some kind of delusion? The sense in which it is a delusion must be one which depends on a claim that, *if* I were to come to know something about the functional properties of this form of consciousness, I would no longer retain it. The form of consciousness qualifies as 'false' or a delusion because my retaining it depends in some way on my being in ignorance of or having false beliefs about its functional properties.

III. The third major way to answer the question, In virtue of what is a form of consciousness an ideology?, is: In virtue of some of its genetic properties, that is, by virtue of some facts about its origin, genesis, or history, about how it arises or comes to be acquired or held by agents, or in virtue of the motives agents have for adopting and acting on it.

Thus, Runciman claims that for the later Engels a form of consciousness is ideologically false in virtue of the fact that the 'beliefs and attitudes' which compose it are 'related in a causal sense to the social situation and thereby to the interests of the believer.'[42] So, presumably, a form of consciousness is an ideology in virtue of something about its causal history. Karl Mannheim holds a similar view, that forms of consciousness are ideological because they are 'expressions' of the class position of those who hold them, that is, because their origin can be traced to the particular experiences of a particular class in society with its characteristic perceptions, interests, and values.[43] Finally, the analogy between psychoanalysis and social theory which is so dominant in much

[42] Runciman, p. 212. The Engels passage on which this is based is one in a letter to Mehring from 1893 (translated in Tucker, p. 648) which states: 'Ideology is a process accomplished by the so-called thinker consciously, but with false consciousness. The real motive forces impelling him remain unknown to him; otherwise it simply would not be an ideological process.'

[43] Mannheim, pp. 55ff, 77ff.

of the work of the members of the Frankfurt School suggests that ideologies might be construed as 'collective rationalisations,' i.e. as systems
of beliefs and attitudes accepted by the agents for reasons which they
could not acknowledge.[44] But what does 'could not' mean here?

   This genetic approach seems to pose more problems for the understanding than did the functional approach.[45] Why should anything we
might learn about the origin, motivation, or causal history of a form of
consciousness give us (rational) grounds for rejecting it, much less for
rejecting it as 'false consciousness' or as a 'delusion?' Of course, if the
form of consciousness has an unsavory causal history this might make
us very *suspicious* of it – we may examine the beliefs it contains with
more than our usual care and may think twice about the implications of
adopting the attitudes – but that doesn't in itself give us good grounds
to reject the form of consciousness. Also if a form of consciousness is an
'expression' of the class-position of a group in society not merely in the
sense that it 'arose out of their experience' but also in the sense that it
is *appropriate only* to those who share that class-position, e.g. if it speaks
only to their particular needs, problems, and values, then it may be
irrelevant to those of us who do not share that class-position. But to say
that it is irrelevant to us is not to say that it is a delusion – it certainly
wouldn't seem to be any kind of delusion for *them;* if we *do* reject it, it is
because it is 'not appropriate' for us and that is something we may determine without any knowledge of its causal history. The causal history
may explain *why* it is inappropriate, but the causal history isn't itself the
grounds for rejecting it; its inappropriateness is.

   By now there is a long history of criticism of the 'genetic fallacy' –
one hasn't shown anything about the truth or falsity of a belief by showing how it arose, one must clearly distinguish 'context of discovery'
from 'context of justification.' If the genetic approach to ideology in the
pejorative sense is to get off the ground, it must somehow show that the
'genetic fallacy,' granted its validity for scientific statements, is *not* necessarily a fallacy for forms of consciousness.

   I have already tipped my hand as to how this argument might proceed. When speaking of the analogy between psychoanalysis and social
theory above, I said that ideologies might be understood as systems of
beliefs and attitudes accepted by the agents for reasons or motives
which those agents *could* not acknowledge. Suppose I have a belief, attitude, or habit of action which I have adopted and cultivate for unacknowledged and unacceptable motives; perhaps I have adopted and
cultivate a habit of virtuous action of a certain sort for completely nar-

[44] TW 159f [T1 311].
[45] Mannheim, pp. 271ff, 283ff, 286f, 291ff.

cissistic reasons which I don't acknowledge and which I would find unacceptable. Even though my motives or reasons for acting in the way I do may be unacceptable, the habit of action may be a habit of virtuous action, i.e. I may consistently do the right thing for the wrong reasons. In this case, coming to acknowledge and recognize my own motives may in fact bring *me* to stop cultivating the habit of action, but then again it may not, and in either case the habit of action may remain the right habit of action for me to cultivate, and I may still recognize that it is the right habit (although I may cease to have the strong motivation I had to continue to cultivate it). But in the case of 'ideologies' it isn't just that they are said to have been adopted for *unacknowledged* motives or reasons, but for motives which *could* not be acknowledged by the agents. This presumably means that *if* the agents had to recognize and acknowledge that *these* were their motives, they would thereby not only no longer be motivated as strongly as they were to continue to accept the ideology, but they would see that there is *no* reason for them to accept it.

One might wonder whether cases like this really exist – cases in which the *only* motive or reason for adopting a form of consciousness is a motive which *cannot* be acknowledged – and one might also legitimately ask for further clarification of the sense in which a motive 'cannot' be acknowledged. Finally one might wonder whether this kind of analysis can be extended to other cases involving the 'causal history' or 'origin and genesis' of a form of consciousness. But *if* these potential objections can be deflected, there might be a chance of showing that the genetic approach to ideology can yield a sense of ideology as delusion or false consciousness. The form of consciousness is false in that it requires ignorance or false belief on the part of the agents of their true motives for accepting it.

So the term 'ideology' is used in a pejorative sense to criticise a form of consciousness because it incorporates beliefs which are false, or because it functions in a reprehensible way, or because it has a tainted origin. I will call these three kinds of criticism: criticism along the epistemic, the functional, and the genetic dimensions respectively.[46] It is

---

[46] Niklas Luhmann sums up some of the standard views about ideology (before dismissing them all) thus: 'Nicht in der kausalen Berwirktheit liegt das Wesen der Ideologie, auch nicht in der instrumentellen Verwendbarkeit bei der es nicht um Wahrheit, sondern um Wirkungen geht, und schließlich auch nicht darin, daß sie die eigentlichen Motive verbirgt' (p. 57). Of these the first and third refer to the 'genetic' dimension, and the second to the 'functional.' Habermas criticises Luhmann because his functionalist theory of ideology leaves no room for a sense in which ideology could be 'false,' i.e. for lacking an analysis of the 'epistemic dimension' (TG 239ff). As will become clearer later, the reason Habermas insists that it must be possible to call an ideology 'false' is that he thinks this is the only way to avoid a kind of pernicious relativism.

extremely important to determine which of these three modes of criticism is basic to a theory of ideology – does the theory start with an
epistemology, with a theory of the proper functioning of society and of
which forms of social organisation are reprehensible, or with a theory
of which 'origins' of forms of consciousness are acceptable and which
unacceptable? Still, although one or another of these three modes of
criticism may be basic, interesting theories of ideology will be ones
which assert some connection between two or more of the three modes.
One of the senses in which the Critical Theory is said by its proponents
to be 'dialectical' (and hence superior to its rivals) is just in that it explicitly connects questions about the 'inherent' truth or falsity of a form
of consciousness with questions about its history, origin, and function
in society.

3   IDEOLOGY IN THE POSITIVE SENSE

The descriptive and explanatory project outlined in section 1 and the
critical project discussed in section 2 are not the only two research programs in which a concept of 'ideology' might come to figure. It isn't just
a neutral fact about human groups that each has a 'culture' or 'socio-
cultural system,' a set of characteristic attitudes, habits, beliefs, modes
of artistic expression, perhaps even a characteristic world-view; participating in a culture is a way of satisfying certain very deep-seated human needs. Humans have a vital need for the kind of 'meaningful' life
and the kind of identity which is possible only for an agent who stands
in relation to a culture.[47] Traditional religious world-views owe their
persistence to their ability to meet some of these basic needs. They do
this by providing agents with approved models of action, goals, ideals,
and values, and by furnishing interpretations of such important existential features of human life as birth and death, suffering, evil, etc. In
addition to such basic existential needs, human agents and groups have
more mundane needs, wants, and interests which a given set of habits,
beliefs, and attitudes, a given 'culture,' can satisfy more or less adequately. Starting, then, from the wants, needs, interests, and the objective situation of a given human group, we can set ourselves the task of
determining what kind of socio-cultural system or what world-view
would be most appropriate for that group, i.e. what 'ideology' (in some
descriptive sense of the term) is most likely to enable the members of
the group to satisfy their wants and needs and further their interests. I

---

[47] Vide 'Können komplexe Gesellschaften eine vernünftige Identität ausbilden?' (in ZR),
sections V, VI, and VII of 'Bewußtmachende oder rettende Kritik – Die Aktualität Walter
Benjamins' (in KK), sections II. 6 and 7 and III. 4 of LS, and TG pp. 163f.

will call this the task of producing for the group an 'ideology in the positive or laudatory sense.' Ideology in this sense is quite different from ideology in either the descriptive or the pejorative senses. Whereas an ideology in any of the descriptive senses is something one *finds* (or perhaps postulates hypothetically for explanatory purposes), and an ideology in the pejorative sense is something one finds and isolates in order to criticize, an ideology in the positive sense isn't something 'out there' to be found by even the most careful empirical investigation. It might be a desideratum for a particular society that it have an ideology in this sense, but the ideology is something *to be* constructed, created, or invented; it is a *verité à faire.*[48]

Possibly the first sketch of this program of constructing an ideology in the positive sense for a human group occurs in Lenin's *What is to be Done?*[49] Here Lenin argues that the beliefs and attitudes most of the members of the working class actually have are *not* beliefs and attitudes appropriate to their objective situation. Not only doesn't the proletariat now have a set of beliefs and attitudes which will enable it to satisfy its basic needs and further its vital interests, but left to its own devices ('spontaneously') it won't ever develop an appropriate form of consciousness; at best it can aspire to a trade-union consciousness which is a debased form of 'bourgeois ideology.'[50] The correct proletarian world-view must be introduced into the proletariat from the outside by the members of a vanguard party (many of whom may well be of bourgeois origin). When Lenin calls upon party intellectuals to help 'the labour movement ... elaborate ... an independent ideology for itself,'[51] he is obviously not using the term 'ideology' in a descriptive sense. He is not calling on them to find out what beliefs and attitudes those in the labor movement actually have – to elaborate *them* would merely yield some further form of 'bourgeois ideology.' Nor is he using the term in a pejorative sense – he is not suggesting that party intellectuals disseminate some form of false consciousness among the working class. The 'independent ideology for the labor movement' is the set of those attitudes and beliefs which would best enable the workers to restructure society in their own interest.

If we are looking for a characterization of it that will make 'positive ideology' a separate category, distinct from ideology in the pejorative sense, it isn't sufficient to say that a positive ideology enables the agents effectively to satisfy some of their needs and desires. First, there must be some restrictions on the kinds of wants, desires, and interests a positive ideology is to satisfy – we will want to exclude overtly sadistic desires, desires to enslave, exploit, or dominate others, etc. Then there must also be some restrictions on the way in which the needs and desires of the group are satisfied – we will probably want to disallow conscious or empirical falsehoods or patently inconsistent beliefs, inculcation of attitudes of hysteria or paranoia, etc. Suppose that the members of some group have very strong aggressive desires, and suppose further that they cling hysterically to a set of patently false beliefs which focus their hostility on the members of some powerless minority. This set of beliefs may be quite effective in enabling them to satisfy their aggressive desires without fear of retaliation, but if we allow it to count as an 'ideology in the positive sense,' the distinction between an ideology in the positive sense and an ideology in the pejorative sense will become blurred.

In certain cases the problems which make these further restrictions on the notion of ideology in the positive sense necessary may not arise. Thus Lukács argues in *Geschichte und Klassenbewußtsein* that the beliefs which would enable the members of the proletariat of a capitalist society to further their own interests most effectively are precisely those beliefs which would comprise a 'scientifically correct' account of capitalist society.[52] Furthermore, the 'correct' beliefs are not merely 'useful' to the proletariat in a general way, they are indispensable – a 'vital necessity' – if the proletariat is to reorganize the whole of society in its own interest. The first part of this claim might seem to be a triviality – what could be more obvious than that agents will generally be more effective in realizing their interests if they have true beliefs – but for Lukács it is by no means a triviality. He holds that, in contrast to the proletariat, the bourgeoisie could and can act to further its interests 'unconsciously' or under the influence of one or another form of false consciousness. Thus, a political order suitable for the maximal development of the capitalist mode of production was created in the English Civil Wars by members of the incipient bourgeoisie in the course of pursuing various religious fantasies. The more the members of the bourgeoisie know about the true nature of capitalist society, the less effective they will be in the class struggle, because the more hopeless they will realize their situation to be in the long run.[53] So the bourgeoisie, paradoxically enough, has an interest in being self-deceived.

If, then, the distinction between ideology in the positive sense and

[52] Lukács, pp. 87, 151f, 357f.
[53] Lukács, pp. 87, 141, 148ff, 357f. Vide infra pp. 85f.

ideology in the pejorative sense is not as sharp as one might have hoped, this is partly a reflection of the fact that historically satisfaction of one's interests and oppression, pursuit of a sense of identity and false consciousness have been all but inextricably linked. Thus, the major way in which ideologies (in the pejorative sense) have traditionally maintained themselves is by harnessing what are in themselves perfectly legitimate human aspirations, such as the desire for a sense of collective identity, so as to create a situation in which the agents can satisfy legitimate existential needs only on condition of accepting the repression the ideological world-view imposes.[54]

The preceding discussion has been artificially simplified by the tacit assumption that the agents' wants, needs, desires, and interests are relatively fixed, as if we could isolate them and hold them constant while asking which of one or another proposed 'ideology' would satisfy a larger number of them to a greater extent. Perhaps the 'existential' needs mentioned above are needs all humans have, but they are quite abstract and even the concrete forms those needs will take in different human societies will vary considerably. Certainly most other human desires, wants, and needs are notoriously variable. A proposed ideology may generate new wants and interests. Some of these may be an acknowledged part of the ideology; others may arise as indirect and perhaps even unintended consequences of adopting the ideology. But a proposed ideology may also deny standing to certain wants, desires, and needs the agents to whom it is addressed in fact have; it may enjoin those who adopt it to stop attempting to gratify these desires or even to try to suppress or eliminate them in themselves. Thus, Christianity breaking into the ancient world doesn't only present itself as a set of beliefs and practices which will satisfy certain human needs and longings; it also articulates and fosters the development of a whole new set of desires, wants, and needs, and anathematizes the satisfaction and further cultivation of various recognized and highly regarded needs and desires, e.g. desire for self-assertion, honor, fame, reputation. It is merely naive to assume that one can construct a 'typical' agent in the Roman Empire in the time of Augustine, determine that agent's wants, needs, and interests, and then comparatively evaluate the extent to which civic humanism, Manicheanism, Platonism, various mystery religions, and Christianity respectively would 'satisfy' these given needs and desires. The course of individual development the *Confessions* describes is quite complex and we have no reason to believe that the process of determining what would be a 'suitable' ideology for some human group would be any less complex. We will have to return to this question at the end of the third chapter.

4 IDEOLOGIEKRITIK

The members of the Frankfurt School hold three theses about Ideologiekritik:

1. Radical criticism of society and criticism of its dominant ideology (Ideologiekritik) are inseparable; the ultimate goal of all social research should be the elaboration of a critical theory of society of which Ideologiekritik would be an integral part.
2. Ideologiekritik is not just a form of 'moralizing criticism,' i.e. an ideological form of consciousness is not criticised for being nasty, immoral, unpleasant, etc. but for being false, for being a form of delusion. Ideologiekritik is itself a cognitive enterprise, a form of knowledge.
3. Ideologiekritik (and hence also the social theory of which it is a part) differs significantly in cognitive structure from natural science, and requires for its proper analysis basic changes in the epistemological views we have inherited from traditional empiricism (modelled as it is on the study of natural science).

In this section I will discuss various ways in which Ideologiekritik might proceed, with particular attention to the questions: (a) In what sense is the particular kind of Ideologiekritik under discussion cognitive? (b) In what sense would a proper account of the kind of Ideologiekritik under discussion require revisions in our inherited epistemology? The forms of Ideologiekritik I will discuss in this section will all focus very narrowly on one of the three modes of criticism.

I. To begin with the first mode of Ideologiekritik – criticism along the epistemic dimension – to what extent can this kind of criticism be accommodated within a traditional empiricist framework? The members of the Frankfurt School take what they call 'positivism' to be the most consistent, plausible modern version of empiricism.

The Frankfurt School's 'positivist' begins by identifying:

(a) those statements or propositions which are potentially true or false;
(b) those statements or propositions which have 'cognitive content' (i.e. which, if true, would be 'knowledge');
(c) those statements or propositions which can be rationally assessed (i.e. which are warrantedly acceptable or rejectable).

Statements without 'cognitive content' are not true or false, but (cognitively) meaningless, and there is no sense in which they can be rationally discussed and evaluated. The positivist program gets its bite from its second step in which it identifies (a) through (c) above with:

(d) those statements or propositions which are scientifically testable;
(e) those statements or propositions which have observational content.[55]

The identification of (d) with (a) through (c) may be called 'scientism' – roughly, the view that the only rationality is scientific rationality;[56] the identification of (e) with (a) through (c) means that only statements with observational content are even potentially 'knowledge,' and that only they are subject to rational discussion and evaluation.

So the positivist, when confronted with a form of consciousness, can subject it to two kinds of criticism:

(a) scientific criticism: reject those beliefs in the form of consciousness which are empirically false or not well-supported;
(b) 'positivist Ideologiekritik': separate clearly 'cognitive' from 'non-cognitive' beliefs; reject all (second-order) beliefs which attribute to non-cognitive beliefs cognitive standing.

Of the four modes of epistemic criticism[57] (the positivist would claim) objectification mistakes and self-fulfilling beliefs will fall to (a) above: an objectification mistake is an empirically false belief – it falsely takes a state of affairs to hold simpliciter, which in fact holds only conditionally upon a particular kind of human social action – and a self-fulfilling belief is not well-supported – its evidence is tainted, but the taint can be discovered by further empirical investigation. The third of the four modes – confusion of epistemic standing – clearly falls under (b) above, but the fourth, confusion of a particular for a general interest, seems quite beyond the scope of positivist criticism.

None of the members of the Frankfurt School thinks that the tasks circumscribed by the positivist are insignificant ones – it is important that people not accept beliefs which are factually erroneous and don't take normative statements to be descriptive – but the positivist's notion of 'rationality' is too narrow and restricted, and can't handle any of the more interesting cases of ideological delusion; by excluding normative

[55] When the members of the Frankfurt School speak of 'the positivists' they have in mind primarily the Vienna Circle. But obviously the discussion in the text doesn't represent their views fully. The members of the Frankfurt School have no views on or interest in logic or mathematics, so I am going to ignore them in formulating 'positivism.'
[56] Cf. EI 13 [T1 4f].
[57] Vide supra, pp. 13ff.

and metaphysical beliefs, preferences, attitudes, etc. from the realm of rational discussion and evaluation, the positivist leaves us without guidance about important parts of our form of consciousness, and thereby abandons whole areas of our life to mere contingent taste, arbitrary decision, and sheer irrationality.[58] But how do we know that taste, preference, and decision aren't the best we can do as guides to what attitudes, normative beliefs, etc. we should adopt? How do we know it isn't just wishful thinking to think that we can have some kind of normative knowledge, or attain some rational set of preferences and attitudes?

We are perhaps not yet in a position to say positively what the 'wider notion of rationality' which will have application to normative beliefs, attitudes, and preferences is, but Habermas believes that inspection of the actual practice of positivist 'Ideologiekritik' will show that positivists are tacitly using a more extensive notion of 'rationality' than they can admit.[59] Positivist Ideologiekritik operates, it will be recalled, by exposing non-cognitive beliefs (e.g. value judgments) which are masquerading as cognitive. In itself this process need not lead to any changes in the substantive views of the agents. If I think that Haydn is a 'better' composer than Friedrich the Great and misconstrue this belief as a cognitive one, the positivist can enlighten me. I will then presumably learn that my original belief is actually a composite of: (a) a belief that the works of Haydn usually instantiate certain properties to a greater degree than do those of Friedrich the Great, and (b) a value judgment that those properties are the properties which make a work of music

---

[58] TP 316–21 [T4 263–8]. This is the weakest (and also the most plausible) of three views critical of positivism to be found in the works of the members of the Frankfurt School:

    (a) strongest view: positivism (and empiricism) do not give an acceptable account even of natural science;

    (b) strong view: positivism gives a correct account of natural science, but (given the nature of the subject-matter) is inadequate as an account of a theory of human society aimed at correct explanation and accurate prediction;

    (c) weak view: positivism gives a correct account of natural science, and of the 'empirical-analytic' part of social theory (i.e. that aimed at correct explanation and prediction), but social theory *also* has a critical part – one aimed at something other than correct explanation and prediction – and of this positivism can give *no* account.

Marcuse holds (a); Habermas explicitly rejects (a) (TW 50–60 [T5 82–91].) Natural science he simply gives away to the positivist. However he confuses (b) and (c). It isn't clear whether he is claiming:

    (1) even to the extent to which natural and social sciences *share* the common goal of explanation and prediction, the peculiar nature of the subject-matter of the social sciences means that these goals can be successfully attained only by the use of methods very different from those used in natural science;

    (2) natural science and social theory differ radically in their cognitive goals, and so in their characteristic methods;

or whether he is claiming some combination of both. In the text I hold to (c).

[59] TP 321 [T4 268].

'good.' Even if I were to accept the claim that (b) is a *mere* preference, utterly without any rational standing, I would still continue to prefer the music of Haydn to that of Friedrich the Great.

But in some cases coming to know that I have made a mistake in the epistemic standing of a belief will cause me to give the belief up. In fact, in some cases there may be noncognitive beliefs, preferences, etc. which *require* to be accepted that they be mistaken for cognitive beliefs. But in what sense can a preference or a normative belief 'require' that the agents who accept it mistake it for a cognitive belief? What might be intended here are cases of the guidance or justification of action; we might think that for certain kinds of action only cognitive beliefs, not beliefs expressive of mere preferences, are acceptable as sources of guidance and legitimation. But if the only reason we hold the belief is that we (falsely) think that it is a cognitive belief, then when we are enlightened about its epistemic standing, we will give it up. After all, I may not share the preference expressed in the belief. Of course this is precisely the reason why anyone would bother to present a preference or value judgment disguised as a cognitive belief — agents will feel compelled to accept a true cognitive belief in a way in which they will not feel compelled to accept my preferences.[60] If upon enlightenment I do give the belief up (because I don't share the preference on which it is based), Habermas wants to say that I have not just changed my beliefs, but that I have moved to a more rational set of beliefs.

The effectiveness and significance of positivist Ideologiekritik depends on the fact that people *do* change their beliefs in the way described above; the positivists can *count* on people giving up beliefs which have been shown *not* to be cognitive, but to be expressions of preferences which cannot be acknowledged publicly as grounds for action. Positivist Ideologiekritik can have the right effect, then, but cannot give an account of its own activity in bringing that effect about. The motivation of the program must be to free agents from irrational belief and action by causing them to give up beliefs based on preferences those agents could not acknowledge; but the positivists can't admit that the motivation of the program is rational (since there aren't any 'rational motivations') or that the effect is to make the agents more rational. So

---

[60] Note that this might be something like an 'objectification mistake' too. Our preferences, attitudes, etc. are somehow more the result of our own activity – we have more control over them than we do over what beliefs will be 'objectively true' of the world. Earlier members of the Frankfurt School were particularly terrified by fascism because they perceived it as *openly* acknowledging that its politics was one of the naked exercise of power, based on arbitrary acts of will. This mode of Ideologiekritik, then, would have nothing to unmask.

positivists can't justify their own activity of criticising ideologies except as a personal preference or an arbitrary decision.[61]

To this the positivist may reply that the fact that people do change their beliefs as described in the last paragraph is no grounds for saying that they have thereby become more rational, acquired a more 'justified' or 'truer' or more 'warranted' set of beliefs. What they have done is to bring their beliefs, preferences, and value judgments into closer agreement with the rest of their non-cognitive beliefs, e.g. beliefs about which preferences they 'ought' to allow themselves to express or by which they 'ought' to allow themselves to be moved. From the fact that the resulting set of beliefs, preferences, etc. is more coherent and consistent, it doesn't follow that it is 'knowledge,' or 'true.' Furthermore, it is sheer defamation to claim that positivists need consider their own activity a mere 'arbitrary' decision; to say that an activity is not grounded on some 'substantial concept of human rationality' (whatever that might mean) is not to say that it is based on some *arbitrary* decision. It isn't 'arbitrary' if it is motivated by deep-seated human needs, an expression of concern for human suffering, etc. But that doesn't make this decision one 'motivated by reason itself' – it is motivated by perfectly understandable and unexceptionable human desires. The decision to eat when one is very hungry is not arbitrary – I couldn't equally well have decided to go swimming – but that doesn't make eating a form of knowledge.

The task then for the members of the Frankfurt School is to give an account of what it means to say that the agents 'could not acknowledge' certain motives which shows how this means something more than that they in general don't like to acknowledge these motives, and to give an account of what it means to say that a belief *'requires'* mistaken belief about its epistemic standing, which means more than just *'if* the agents are enlightened about their mistake, they will *in fact* give the belief up.' In what sense is it irrational to act on motives which one 'could not' acknowledge or to hold value judgments or preferences which 'require' mistakes about their epistemic standing?

In a way the oddest thing about this whole discussion is the extent to which Habermas is himself infected with the positivism against which he is struggling. In my reconstruction of the positivists' position I claimed that positivists tacitly identified statements which are potentially true or false (a), statements which have cognitive content (b), and statements on which there could be a rational consensus (c).[62] The pos-

[61] Cf. TP 32of [T4 267f].
[62] Vide supra pp. 26f., infra pp. 88f.

itivists then went on to argue that all rationality was scientific rationality (d), and that all scientifically meaningful statements were statements with observational content (e). Since attitudes, preferences, value judgments, normative beliefs, etc. obviously have no direct observational content, they can't be true or false, hence they are cognitively meaningless, so there are strong limits to rational discussion of them, and ultimately one can have no warrant for adopting or acting on them; any consistent set of preferences, attitudes, etc. is as good, as 'rational,' as any other.

Habermas counters in the obvious way: Clearly not any consistent set of preferences, attitudes, and normative beliefs is as 'rational' as any other. This sense of 'rational' may be unclear and difficult to analyse, but that doesn't mean that it is illicit or doesn't exist, and if positivism can't give an account of it, so much the worse for positivism. But instead of going on to attack the first part of the positivists' view – the identification of (a) through (c) – Habermas accepts it; so, if some normative beliefs are more rational than others, there must be a kind of normative knowledge; because some preferences and attitudes are more rational than others, sets of preferences and attitudes can be 'true' or 'false.' 'Truth' and 'falsity' as used in science do not admit of degrees; a proposition is true or false, and *tertium non datur*. But rationality is not like that. Decisions, preferences, attitudes, etc. can be more or less rational; agents can have stronger or weaker warrant for their actions, can be more or less aware of their own motives, can be more or less enlightened in their normative beliefs. If I am asked whether I agree with Habermas or with the positivists, that is, whether I think that there is a single, 'true,' uniquely rational set of human preferences, attitudes, and normative beliefs, or whether I think that there is *no* sense in which any set of attitudes, preferences, and normative beliefs is 'more rational' than any other, the only reasonable reply is to reject this alternative as falsely posed.

II. With that I turn to the second approach to Ideologiekritik, that in terms of the functional properties of forms of consciousness. An ideology is a world-picture which stabilizes or legitimizes domination.[63] But

---

[63] Vide TG 245, 247, 257, 259, 279, 285f, 289f. I won't discuss the second and third functional senses of ideology, i.e. 'an ideology is a form of consciousness which serves to mask social contradictions,' and 'an ideology is a form of consciousness which hinders maximal development of the forces of production (cf. supra, p. 18.)

In some cases 'masking social contradictions' may be a way of supporting or legitimizing an oppressive social order, so a form of consciousness which is an ideology in that it masks social contradictions will also be an ideology in the sense that it supports or legitimizes 'Herrschaft'.

what is the relation between the 'falsity' of the form of consciousness and its functioning to support or legitimize oppression?[64] There are four possibilities:

A. The world-picture is false and it stabilizes or legitimizes oppression, but its falsity and its oppressive functioning have no inherent connection. We can know that it is false independently of knowing whether it functions oppressively, and we can know that it functions oppressively independently of knowing whether or not it is false.[65]

B. The world-picture is false – we assume from the start that we have whatever grounds are necessary for asserting that – and the judgment that the world-picture functions oppressively is parasitic on our judgment that it is false. Consider the following case: Suppose we have a world-picture, a central part of which is a set of normative beliefs which are used to give legitimacy to the basic institutions of the society. Like most social institutions, these will be likely to have repressive features; the question then is whether this is necessary or legitimate repression, or whether it is oppression, domination, Herrschaft, etc. One way to answer this question would be to look at the arguments given for the legitimacy of the institution; if these arguments are correct and start from 'true' normative beliefs, the institution (and the repression associated with it) is justified, if the 'best' available arguments must start from false normative beliefs, the institution is not justified, and, if in addition it imposes frustration of given human preferences, it is a form of oppression. So to know whether what the world-picture supports and legitimizes is 'Herrschaft' or oppression one must know whether the world-picture is itself true or false.

This answer won't work, of course, but it points in the right direction. From the fact that the best arguments the members of the society can

---

[64] As section 2, part II of this chapter indicates there are various quite different views about what exactly it is that an ideology in the functional sense stabilizes or legitimates: repression, Herrschaft, illegitimate repression, Zwangsverhältnisse (TG 247), surplus repression, etc. I will use the term 'oppression' and its derivatives (e.g. 'functions oppressively') in the following as a place-holder for whatever reprehensible feature of society 'ideology' is defined as stabilizing and legitimating.

[65] At TP 310 [T4 257] Habermas speaks of ideological error in a way which combines all three approaches to ideology: 'Der Irrtum, mit dem es die Aufklärung zu tun hatte, ist vielmehr das falsche Bewußtsein einer Epoche, das in den Institutionen einer falschen Gesellschaft verankert ist, und ihrerseits herrschende Interessen befestigt.' So ideological consciousness is:
    (a) epistemically false (i.e. it is an 'Irrtum');
    (b) functionally reprehensible (i.e. it 'befestigt herrschende Interessen');
    (c) genetically unacceptable (i.e. it is 'in den Institutionen einer falschen Gesellschaft verankert').
Although it is hard to be sure, it would seem as if Habermas means here that these three things are independent of each other.

give are not valid, it doesn't follow that there *are* no valid arguments to the legitimacy of the institution. So the judgment that *this* world-picture is oppressive is not parasitic on a judgment that *it* is false, but it may depend on a claim that no true world-picture could yield valid arguments for the legitimacy of the institutions, or – if one wishes to adhere strictly to the principle that Ideologiekritik is a form of 'internal criticism' – that no true world-picture 'acceptable' or 'accessible' to the agents could yield valid arguments for the legitimacy of the social institutions.[66]

C. We can reverse B and give philosophical primacy not to the epistemic properties of the world-picture, but to its functional properties: A world-picture or form of consciousness is 'false' in virtue of the fact that what it stabilizes or legitimizes are relations of Herrschaft.

It is hard to see how this could work in this simple form. A form of consciousness might contain (among other things) some simple descriptive beliefs; if these are observationally accurate, why call them 'false,' whatever their functional properties. To use 'false' in this 'functional' sense of descriptive beliefs could cause nothing but confusion; the same belief might turn out both (observationally accurate and hence) 'true' and (functionally) 'false.' But I assume that the whole point of the use of words like 'true' or 'false' is that they represent a definitive judgment on whether a belief is to be rejected or accepted,[67] so we want to avoid cases in which we say of the same belief that it is both true and false.

Still we may be able to salvage this 'functional' sense for a world-picture or form of consciousness as a whole. If one thinks of the characteristic components of a form of consciousness as attitudes, preferences, and normative and metaphysical beliefs, one might claim that these have no clear observational content to get in the way. We might wish to express a definitive judgment on their acceptability by calling them

---

[66] With this terminological distinction between 'acceptable' and 'accessible' I want to signal a difference between what the agents would adopt if it were presented to them, and what they could reasonably be expected to develop themselves in their historical situation.

[67] Vide supra pp. 31ff, infra pp. 94ff. Some members of the Frankfurt School, notably Adorno (vide my review of *Negative Dialektik* in the *Journal of Philosophy*, 1975), may hold the Hegelian view that a statement or form of consciousness can be both true and false. Fortunately I need not try to explicate this difficult and obscure doctrine, because, as his paper on truth (WT) makes clear, Habermas does not wish to adopt this usage. Even in his early works in which the traces of Hegel are most marked, Habermas avoids saying directly that ideological consciousness is *both* true *and* false. Thus in the book review 'Literaturbericht zur philosophischen Diskussion um Marx und den Marxismus' published in 1957 (reprinted TP 387ff) he says that ideological consciousness may be a 'correct' or 'accurate' representation of reality, but is 'false:' 'Es selbst [scil. das Bewußtsein] wird falsch durch die – sogar richtige – Spiegelung einer falschen Wirklichkeit. . . . [die Ideologie findet] ihre äußerste Grenze in der korrekten Abbildung des falschen Bestehenden' (TP 437). Cf. O'Neill, p. 236.

'false' if they stabilize or legitimize relations of 'Herrschaft'; otherwise, true. We needn't worry that this will conflict with our judgment on their descriptive accuracy; there won't be any. So the judgment that a world-picture or form of consciousness is 'ideologically false' (on this view) is a judgment passed on the form of consciousness as a whole in virtue of the way in which the characteristic attitudes, preferences and normative and metaphysical beliefs which make up the form of consciousness function in the society.[68]

One might take it as a great advantage of this approach that which forms of consciousness are ideologically false will change over time and depend on details of the particular historical situation; the same set of beliefs and attitudes may in some historical epochs support repressive social structures and in others may not.[69] Thus, what were originally 'idle' metaphysical speculations about the nature of 'o'ʋσία' with no social function at all, save perhaps to provide Greek gentlemen with a post-prandial conversational alternative to the flute-girls,[70] may in a different historical context be absorbed into Christian theology and acquire a repressive function.

If, however, we are going to use the reprehensible functioning of a world-picture to define its ideological falsity, we must have a very clear idea of which modes of functioning are reprehensible. This brings us back to the old question: Is the form of consciousness reprehensible (i.e. ideological) if it functions to support or legitimize Herrschaft, surplus repression, surplus Herrschaft, illegitimate repression, etc.?[71]

'Herrschaft' the reader will recall, was defined relative to the ability to frustrate agents' wants and preferences.[72] 'Macht' (power) is the ability to impose on agents the frustration of their preferences, or, as Habermas puts it in Theorie der Gesellschaft, Macht is the ability to prevent others from pursuing their interests.[73] The exercise of Macht is repression. This exercise is either 'manifest' – open use of force or direct threat to use force – or 'normative.' Repression is 'normative' if the agents are prevented from pursuing their interests by a set of norma-

---

[68]"One needn't even deny that the form of consciousness might contain some simple descriptive beliefs; these remain true or false in the normal empirical sense regardless of the 'ideological' judgment on the form of consciousness as a whole.

[69]The same is true of other 'functional' approaches, i.e. of the definition of ideology as what serves to hide social contradictions and the definition of ideology as what hinders maximal development of the forces of production.

[70]The αυλός of course was not a flute – it had a double reed – but in this case mistranslation may have aesthetic advantages. Imagine Alkibiades' entrance at the end of the Symposium 'drunk, crowned, and supported by a female oboist.'

[71]Vide supra pp. 15–18.

[72]Vide supra p. 16.

[73]TG 254.

tive beliefs they accept. 'Normative power' if distributed 'asymmetrically' is 'Herrschaft.'

The appeal of the notion of 'surplus repression' (and of the notion of 'surplus Herrschaft') derives from the hope that it would provide us with an 'objective' standard for evaluating societies and their associated forms of consciousness – we might even be able to measure the 'surplus repression' in a given society at least approximately and comparatively. But to measure the amount of 'surplus repression' in a society we would have to determine what the wants, needs, preferences, and desires of the members of the society are and what the economy 'requires' to be able to reproduce itself. Unfortunately both of these notions – the 'wants, needs, and desires of the agents' and the 'requirements of the economy' – are highly problematic.

To say that '. . . is required by the economy,' or '. . . is required if the economy is to function' is at best an ellipsis; to say that 'the economy' 'functions' is to say that it functions at some level of efficiency (i.e. at some level of expenditure of resources) to provide some level of satisfaction of a qualitatively specific set of human wants and needs of a quite particular kind; it presumably also means that the industrial plant does not disengorge a mass of goodies and then promptly collapse, so the economy must function in such a way that it not only satisfies certain human wants, but also 'reproduce itself.' One can't even begin to determine whether the society imposes surplus repression on its members unless one specifies *what* level of satisfaction of *what* particular human desires and needs the economy is to provide. Did the ancient economy 'require' the use of slave labor in order to function at a level which would provide each Mikrokles with an onion, a barley cake, and half a cabbage for each of his two meals a day? Or did it require the use of slave labor if it was to function so as to allow Alkibiades to race in a four-horse chariot in the morning and spend the afternoons playing cottabos in the baths? Or would Mikrokles get only one onion a day if Alkibiades spent less time racing? The extra onion then is Mikrokles' share of the 'fruits of Athenian imperialism.'

Associated with every human society there will be a set of 'accepted' wants, 'needs,' and desires, and a traditional level of expected satisfaction of these wants and desires.[74] But one can't define 'surplus repression' as any repression more than that required for the economy to function so as to satisfy the socially accepted wants and 'needs' of the agents at the traditional level. After all, the set of 'accepted' wants, needs, and desires, and the traditional level of consumption may them-

---

[74] Vide Sahlins (1976), Chapters 2 and 3.

selves well be part of the 'ideology' we wish to criticize; appeal to 'surplus repression' was supposed to give us a standpoint *outside* the given social interpretation of the agents' needs, from which to criticize it. On the other hand, no member of the Frankfurt School wishes to argue that the only 'real' wants and needs are those which must be satisfied to insure minimal biological survival, so that any repression more than that needed to insure the physical survival of the agents is 'surplus.' Agents in society have acquired sophisticated cultural needs, and it is as legitimate and important that they be satisfied as it is that the agents get enough food and shelter.[75]

This suggests that 'surplus repression' can't be the starting-point and basis for Ideologiekritik. Rather it seems that one must start with some kind of theory of which needs and wants are legitimate and which ideologically false; the amount of surplus repression, then, is the amount of repression exacted beyond that required to satisfy the agents' legitimate wants and needs. '*This* repression is surplus' is a conclusion which sums up a critical argument; the real work of Ideologiekritik will already have been done in distinguishing legitimate from 'false' wants and needs.

Perhaps we can still find a way to give philosophical primacy to the functional properties of a world-picture, but the notion of 'surplus repression' won't give us a quick and short way to an 'objective' definition of 'oppression.'

D. Finally we might claim that neither the falsity of the world-picture, nor its mode of functioning, have any primacy in the analysis of ideology because they are inherently interconnected. One can't determine that the world-picture is false apart from an argument which at some point crucially appeals to the fact that this world-picture supports or legitimizes admitted oppression, nor can one show that what the world-picture supports or legitimizes *is* in fact oppression without some appeal to the falsity of the world-picture. Since Peirce and Dewey such contextualist views are not completely unknown among English-speaking philosophers; members of the Frankfurt School would probably call this approach 'dialectical.'

III. The third approach to Ideologiekritik is in terms of the genetic properties of forms of consciousness. How can a form of consciousness be 'false' in virtue of something about its origin, history, or genesis?

One widely practiced form of genetic Ideologiekritik is what I will call the 'social origins approach.' In certain forms of vulgar Marxism to

[75]TW 162 [T1 312f].

call a belief a 'bourgeois belief' or a 'feudal belief' is to criticize it as ideologically false because of its social origin, i.c. because it typically or characteristically arises in societies dominated by the bourgeoisie, or because the original proponents of the belief are themselves members of the bourgeoisie.

Prima facie this doesn't seem to be a very promising line of argument. Most nineteenth- and early-twentieth-century natural scientists were working in a society dominated by the bourgeoisie, and perhaps one might argue that their physics was a kind of intellectual enterprise that characteristically arises in bourgeois societies, obsessed as they are with efficient and reliable methods for controlling natural phenomena. Still, although we may explain why particular physicists came to hold a particular false physical theory by reference to their social environment and the 'requirements of bourgeois society,' the theory is not false *because* it arose in a bourgeois society, but because it is inaccurate, incompatible with the evidence, etc. Why should the situation be any different for 'forms of consciousness?'

Proponents of the social origins approach think that the situation is different for forms of consciousness because they hold a very strong view about the connection of the social origins of a form of consciousness and certain other facts about that form of consciousness. They believe that if a form of consciousnesness characteristically arises among the members of a certain social class, that form of consciousness will be the 'expression' of the (class-) position, standpoint, or 'viewpoint' of that class, or, alternatively, that, if a form of consciousness characteristically arises in a society dominated by a particular social class, it will be an 'expression' of the class-position, or standpoint, or viewpoint of that dominant class.[76] To say that a form of consciousness is an expression of the position in society or viewpoint of a social class is to say:

(a) that the form of consciousness formulates the class-interests of that social class,

or,

(b) that the form of consciousness represents social reality as it appears to the members of that social class,

or,

(c) both (a) and (b).

[76] Mannheim, 78ff, 84f, 265ff; Lukács, 127ff.

It is important in (a) above that when we speak of a form of consciousness as the 'expression' of class-position, we mean that it *formulates* the class-interests of that social class, and not merely, for instance, that adopting and acting on that form of consciousness will further the class-interests of some social class. To say that acting on a particular form of consciousness will further the interests of some social class is to attribute to that form of consciousness a 'functional property.' Perhaps one might want in fact to claim that, if a form of consciousness characteristically arises among the members of some class, acting on it will usually in fact foster their class interests, but this may turn out to be a form of 'functional criticism' in disguise, that is, one may not be criticizing the form of consciousness because it arises thus and so, but because given that it arises thus and so it will have these and those functional properties.

What is wrong, though, with 'formulating' or 'fostering' a class-interest; why is this grounds for rejecting a form of consciousness as ideological? It might seem grounds rather for cherishing it. Why isn't a form of consciousness that correctly formulates the interests of a social class an ideology 'in the positive sense?'[77]

The answer is that, although the class-interest of some particular class may in some circumstances be identical with the 'general interest' of the society, very often this will not be the case. But classes have a natural tendency to identify their own particular class interest with the general interest. A form of consciousness is to be rejected if it falsely presents a particular class-interest as the general interest of the society, or if, although purporting to foster the general interest, it in fact fosters the particular interest of a social class.[78]

If this, or something like it, is what is intended by those who criticize a form of consciousness for being 'an expression of the position in society of a particular class,' namely that this form of consciousness falsely presents the particular interest of this particular social class as the general interest, this is *not* a form of genetic Ideologiekritik. The form of consciousness in question is not being criticized in virtue of its origin, but in virtue of the 'falsity' it is likely to have as a result of this origin. Its origin in the particular experiences of a particular social class will then be at best a more or less reliable indicator that the form of consciousness will be found to present a particular class-interest as the general interest. So this purportedly genetic Ideologiekritik is actually a kind of epistemic Ideologiekritik.

Similar conclusions follow if one interprets the statement: 'This form

[77] Vide supra pp. 22–6.
[78] LS 38f, 153ff [T2 22f, 111ff].

of consciousness is an expression of the viewpoint of this particular social class' as meaning 'This form of consciousness represents social reality as it appears to the members of that social class' (as in (b) above). That a form of consciousness represents social reality as it appears to the members of some social class would seem no grounds for rejecting it. But suppose one holds that the 'truth' about society is a 'total' view of that society, i.e. some kind of combination or integration of the ways the society appears from the perspective of *each* of its constituent groups. Then a form of consciousness which represents social reality as it appears to the members of some particular social class is a merely partial view of the society, i.e. it is not the 'truth' about the society, i.e. it is false consciousness.[79] Fortunately it is not necessary to try to cash in the metaphors of this dubious theory of social knowledge; here too, clearly, what is at issue is a form not of genetic but of epistemic Ideologiekritik. What is wrong with ideological forms of consciousness is not their origin, but their false representation of social reality.

So far we have not found any genuinely 'genetic' form of Ideologiekritik. Perhaps we will fare better if we try to take seriously the analogy between Ideologiekritik and psychoanalysis, and between ideologically false consciousness and individual neurosis.[80]

In *Die Zukunft einer Illusion* Freud distinguishes between 'error' ('Irrtum'), 'delusion' ('Wahnidee'), and 'illusion' ('Illusion').[81] An 'Irrtum' is just a normal, everyday, false factual belief, e.g. the belief that Sigmund Freud was born in Vienna is an 'Irrtum.' A 'Wahnidee' is a false belief an agent holds *because* holding this belief satisfies some wish the agent has: e.g. a man who falsely believes that he is Charlemagne because this belief satisfies his wish to be an important historical personage is suffering from a delusion, a 'Wahnidee.' An 'illusion' is a belief which may or may not be false, but which is held by the agent because it satisfies a wish. Freud's example of an 'illusion' is the belief of a middle-class girl that a prince will come and marry her. It may in fact turn out that a prince does come and marry her – in Freud's Vienna there were such princes around, although probably not very many, so the girl's chances were rather slim – but the reason she believes that she will marry a prince is that this belief satisfies some wish she has.

The 'illusion' mentioned in the title of Freud's work is religious belief, but his discussion is not as clear and unambiguous as one might wish. Some religious beliefs are like 'Wahnideen' – patently false beliefs to

[79] Mannheim, 282ff, 103ff.
[80] TW 159f [T1 311f].
[81] Freud, pp. 164f.

which the agents cling because they satisfy some deep needs – but most religious beliefs are merely 'illusions' – beliefs of indeterminate truth-value which are accepted because they satisfy agents' wishes.

But are religious beliefs really 'illusions' in the way in which the middle-class girl's belief about 'her' prince is an illusion? The middle-class girl's belief is of indeterminate truth-value – it may or may not be true – only in the sense that she does not now have any evidence for it. But in itself the belief *is* true or false – either the prince will come or he won't. Freud himself suggests that this is not quite the case with religious beliefs: 'Über den Realitätswert der meisten von ihnen kann man gar nicht urteilen. So wie sie unbeweisbar sind, sind sie auch unwiderlegbar.'[82] This might be taken to mean: We can't *prove* them or disprove them, but we could *in principle* have evidence for them – they are in themselves true or false – it is just that *at the moment* we don't have any evidence for them either way, just as the girl has no evidence for her belief. But it might also mean: We can't make any judgment *at all* about them as representations of reality; they are so vague and unspecific, we wouldn't know what to count as evidence for them – perhaps it is even wrong to think of some of them as purporting to represent reality at all rather than merely expressing certain attitudes. What could be the evidence for a belief that 'there's a destiny that shapes our ends, rough-hew them as we will?' Or for the belief that 'All there is, is either substance or attribute of substance and God is the one substance?' From here it is but a step to the claim that there is no point in calling such things 'true' or 'false.' Preponderance of the evidence *could* be the reason the middle-class girl thinks she will marry a prince (but it probably isn't), but no one could hold these religious beliefs as a result of considering the non-existent or completely inadequate evidence for them, so the reason these beliefs have been able to perpetuate themselves through millennia must be that they satisfy agents' needs and wishes.

So we must distinguish (at least):

(a) cases of delusion: Despite overwhelming evidence that the belief is false, the agent continues to hold it because it satisfies some wish;
(b) cases of illusion in which the belief is one for which the agent *could* have adequate evidence, but which is accepted by the agent *because* it satisfies some wish;
(c) cases of illusion involving beliefs for which there could not be adequate evidence (and which therefore must be accepted because they satisfy some wish).

---

[82] Freud, p. 165.

What are we to say, then, about ideology in the pejorative sense? Is it a kind of delusion or of illusion? Let me start with what I will call the generalized 'wishful thinking model' of Ideologiekritik. According to this model, Ideologiekritik proceeds by showing:

(a) that certain agents make a characteristic kind of mistake
(b) that one can explain why they make that mistake by ultimate reference to interests.

This model differs from normal cases of 'wishful thinking' and from the cases Freud discusses in that the explanation in (b) need not be an explanation in terms of individual psychology. Thus the agents may make the mistake because of the institutional context within which they act, and we may explain why this institutional context has the characteristics it must have in order to produce the mistake by reference to the interests of some agents, but those who make the mistake may not be motivated as individuals to satisfy the interest by reference to which the mistake is explained. In fact, it may not even be the case that the interest by reference to which the mistake is explained is an interest *of* those who make the mistake. Consider, for instance, members of some disadvantaged group who are employed in a government bureau to collect and analyse unemployment statistics. Let us suppose that the rate of unemployment in the society is systematically underestimated and that the ultimate explanation of this fact is that this underestimation is in the interest of some powerful group in the society. The agents in the government bureau who 'make' the mistake may have no interest whatever which is satisfied by holding a false belief about the rate of unemployment – in fact underestimation of the rate of unemployment may be directly contrary to their interests. The way the 'interest' transforms itself into error is not by providing *them* with a direct individual incentive or motive to make the mistake, but by arranging the conditions under which the statistics are collected and evaluated so that rational agents working in those conditions will in general be prone to make this kind of systematic error.

The 'generalized wishful thinking model' described above makes ideology out to be a kind of 'delusion,' a 'Wahnidee.' The belief in question is one which is clearly false, there is ample evidence available for rational agents to see that the belief is false, but they don't, and the reason they don't is that powerful interests are operating to place them in non-standard conditions.

It is, of course, an extremely important task for empirical social research to point out how the interests of powerful social groups cause false information to be produced and disseminated throughout the so-

ciety, but it is not the task of Ideologiekritik. In the case described above
– as in typical cases of what Freud called 'delusion' – the mistake or
error in question was a straightforward factual error. But no amount of
factual error is in itself sufficient to render a form of consciousness
ideologically false. If a form of consciousness *is* ideological, one *result*
might be that certain kinds of truths were systematically overlooked or
certain kinds of errors systematically made. *That* certain kinds of errors
are characteristically made, might lead us to suspect that some 'ideological' element in the form of consciousness would be threatened by correct belief, but this does not mean that ideological falsity *consists* in factual ignorance or false factual belief. On the 'genetic' view under
consideration in this section, the ideological falsity of a form of consciousness is supposed to consist in something about its origin or genesis; Ideologiekritik was to ferret out this peculiar kind of non-empirical
error. But *neither* part of the criticism along the lines of the model of
wishful thinking – neither (a) nor (b) – seems to require any but the
normal empirical methods of social research, and what is wrong about
an underestimation of the rate of employment is not that it has any
particular origin, but that it is an underestimation, i.e. that it is factually
in error.

So, it would seem, if ideological error is 'delusion' in Freud's sense,
or is appropriately analysed in the 'model of wishful thinking' in the
unspecific form in which that model has been presented above, Ideologiekritik is not an activity which requires any revisions in received
views about epistemology.

If ideological error is taken to be like the illusion from which the
middle-class girl in Freud's example suffers, the same argument would
seem to apply. One doesn't show that the *belief* is false by showing that
this person holds it because it satisfies one of her wishes. The way to
criticise the belief is not to show that she wishes it to be true, but to show
how inherently implausible it is, and we do that by 'normal empirical
means.' To this it might be objected that the point here is not to show
that the belief is false, but to criticize the *agent* for adopting an inherently implausible belief for which she had no evidence. But it requires
no major revisions in our epistemology to treat cases like this either;
why is even the positivist estopped from criticizing agents for holding
implausible, empirically unsupported beliefs?

Are ideologies, then, like the second kind of illusion, i.e. like (c) in
my scheme above?[83] That is, are ideologies forms of consciousness with
little or no observational content, which, therefore, if adopted at all,

<hr />

[83] Vide supra, p. 40.

must be adopted because they satisfy some wish, desire or interest of the agents? It can't *in itself* be an objection to a belief that it satisfies a wish or desire, or even that it is accepted because it satisfies a wish or desire. True beliefs for which I have good evidence will satisfy my desire to accept true beliefs for which I have good evidence, and that they satisfy this wish is the reason I accept them. What is wrong with 'wishful thinking' is not that we accept beliefs because they satisfy desires we have, but that we accept these beliefs because they satisfy the wrong, i.e. inappropriate, desires. Empirical beliefs can be accepted because they satisfy our wish to accept well-confirmed empirical beliefs; if we accept them because they satisfy some *other* wish, we are engaging in 'wishful thinking.' This suggests that we might be able to distinguish appropriate and inappropriate motivations for different classes of beliefs. Even if the only appropriate and acceptable motivation for accepting empirical beliefs is the desire to accept only well-confirmed beliefs, this *cannot* be an appropriate motivation for accepting normative and metaphysical beliefs or for adopting attitudes, preferences, etc., since there is no way in principle in which any of these things could be empirically confirmed.

It is just not an option for us as human beings *not* to have some attitudes, preferences, and normative beliefs. Is there some way, then, of distinguishing appropriate and acceptable from inappropriate and unacceptable motives for attitudes, preferences, and non-empirical beliefs? Should preferences, attitudes, etc. be rejected if they have been adopted for unacceptable motives? Are they then to be rejected as 'false?' Empirical beliefs adopted as the result of wishful thinking need not be false; in fact we generally speak of 'wishful thinking' only in cases where the belief is false or at least very implausible. But if 'wishful thinking' just means (as we have taken it to mean) accepting a belief *because* it satisfies some wish (other than the wish to accept well-supported beliefs), there is no reason why we might not have *some* evidence for a belief accepted because of 'wishful thinking,' as long as the evidence is not the reason we accept it. So to criticize agents for indulging in wishful thinking is not necessarily to show that their beliefs are to be rejected as false. This line of argument can't be carried over to preferences, attitudes, and non-empirical beliefs, because with them one can't distinguish their truth or falsity from the motives the agents have for accepting them. Still, this may mean no more than that non-empirical beliefs are not true or false at all (since they are not 'observationally' true or false); it certainly doesn't imply that we show non-empirical beliefs, attitudes, preferences, etc. to be *false* by impugning the motives of those who adopt them.

A prime example of the genetic approach to Ideologiekritik is

Nietzsche's criticism of Christianity.[84] This criticism is 'genetic' because it appeals to a purported fact about the 'origin' of Christianity – that Christianity arises from hatred, envy, resentment, and feelings of weakness and inadequacy. To say that Christianity 'arises' out of hatred and envy is presumably not to make a historical statement – it is unclear what critical import such a statement could have – but to make a general statement about the typical motivation of Christians. How do we know that these motives are 'unacceptable?' Nietzsche, in presenting this criticism, need not himself be committed to the view that hatred is in general, or always, or even ever an unacceptable motive for action. It is sufficient for the critical enterprise that the Christian cannot acknowledge hatred as an acceptable motive for beliefs, preferences, and attitudes. Since it is a central doctrine of Christianity that agents ought to be motivated by love, and not by hatred, resentment, envy, etc., Christianity itself gives the standard of 'acceptability' for motives in the light of which it is criticized. If Nietzsche's account of its 'origins' is correct, Christianity 'requires' of its adherents that they not recognize their own motives for adhering to it. It isn't very important whether one wants to say that this criticism, if correct, shows Christianity to be 'false,' or 'merely' something else – contradictory, radically irrational, unstable, etc. The point is that the Christian who accepts Nietzsche's argument and thereupon gives Christianity up, is not doing anything analogous to acting on a whim, expressing a mere preference, or making an arbitrary decision; this action is rationally grounded.

This example suggests that at least in some cases we can 'criticize' a form of consciousness because of the motives which lead the agents to adopt it. But the 'origin, genesis, and history' of a form of consciousness includes more than just the motives of the agents who adhere to it. Chapter 3 will treat a kind of genetic Ideologiekritik in which a form of consciousness is criticized because of non-motivational features of the conditions under which the agents could have acquired it.

[84] Nietzsche (1969).

2

❧❦

INTERESTS

1 REAL INTERESTS

In Chapter 1 I discussed various ways in which the term 'ideology' has been used; for present purposes the most important of these ways was the use of 'ideology' to refer to 'false consciousness.' In section 4 of Chapter 1 we tried to determine what it meant to say that ideological consciousness was 'false.' But throughout most of Chapter 1 we abstracted from what might seem to be an important substantive specification of ideological error, namely it is supposed to be the case that agents who suffer from ideologically false consciousness are deluded about their own true interests. Ideologiekritik is supposed to 'enlighten' agents about their true interests. In this chapter I will try to determine what it might mean to distinguish the 'true,' or 'real,' or 'objective' interests of agents from their 'merely apparent' or 'merely phenomenal,' or 'perceived' interests, and what might be meant by the claim that a group of agents is deceived or deluded about its true interests.

Up to now I have spoken of the wants, interests, needs, desires, and preferences of a group of agents as if they were all more or less the same thing. We attribute a set of wants, preferences, and desires to a group of agents on the basis of their explicit avowals – that is, on the basis of what they *say* they want – and on the basis of their actual overt behavior. But the avowals may be confused, fragmentary, and contradictory, and may stand in a most tenuous relation to a body of equally confused and conflict-ridden behavior. We neither wish to take what they *say* strictly at face-value despite overwhelming evidence that they *never* act on their avowed 'desires,' nor will we want to ignore completely the fact of human weakness and assume that their sincere assertions are hypocritical, if they don't *always* act on them. So the set of desires and preferences we attribute to the group is a theoretical construct which fills out the fragmentary evidence, removes some of the contradictions between avowals and behavior, and may end up ascribing to the group on the basis of its actual behavior, wants and desires of which no individual member is aware. It will be quite difficult in making this theoretical construct not to impose on the group too determinate and coherent a set of desires; when should apparent contradictions be allowed to stand and what kind of rationality assumptions should be made when smoothing them out? Individuals and groups, then, may be unaware of some of their own desires and preferences, i.e. on the basis of their manifest behavior we may have reason to attribute to them preferences and desires which they not only themselves never articulate, but which they would verbally disavow.

'Needs' are defined relative to the successful functioning of an individual or social organism; if the 'needs' of the organism are not satisfied, it will malfunction. A human being needs a certain minimal intake of calories, protein, vitamins, etc. This means that if a human being does *not* obtain that minimal level of nutrition over an extended period, it will malfunction, become lethargic, have lowered resistance to disease, perhaps die. The notion of 'successful functioning' is quite flexible. If I eat something nourishing and immediately fall over dead, I have obviously malfunctioned, but what if I become slightly lethargic as a result of a marginally inadequate diet?

To extend this account to social 'organisms' will be difficult; the notion of 'successful functioning' is clearly even less well-defined for social systems than it is for biological organisms.[1] When is a society 'healthy' and when 'pathological?'

Agents and societies may not be aware of their needs. To remain with the dietary example, I know that I need a certain amount of vitamin-C over any given six-month period, otherwise I will get scurvy, but there are numerous other dietary substances my body needs in order to function, and I in no way assume that I know that I need all of them.

Agents may or may not have an 'interest' in the satisfaction of their wishes and desires. Partially reformed alcoholics may still have a strong desire for drink, but they also have an interest in the non-satisfaction of that desire. I may have an interest in having some of my desires satisfied, but I may also have an interest in not having them satisfied at the moment (or at all), in acquiring new desires which I do not now have, or in losing desires of which I disapprove. One might try to construe all these cases as ones in which I experience a conflict between two desires – perhaps a 'first-order desire' and a 'second-order desire'[2] – rather than as a conflict between wish/desire on the one hand, and something else ('interest') on the other.[3] I would prefer not to adopt this strategy for the following reason: I may have a desire with which I

---

[1] ZL 176ff, EI 350 [T1 288f], TW 162 [T1 312f], TG 146ff, esp. 151f, 163ff.
[2] Vide Frankfurt (1971).
[3] I have been much influenced in my treatment of interests by Hirschman (1977).

wholly identify myself, and may have an interest in not gratifying that desire, although I have *no* second-order desire not to gratify it. Partially reformed alcoholics have a strong first-order desire for drink, and a strong second-order desire that that first-order desire not be satisfied; these desires conflict. An unregenerate alcoholic has an excessive desire for drink, and *no* appropriate second-order desire that that excessive desire not be satisfied. Perhaps if unregenerate alcoholics were more rational, they *would* try to acquire the appropriate second-order desires, but, from the fact that they would try to acquire them under some other circumstances, it doesn't follow that they now in some sense 'have' them. Note also that I wish to keep the notion of 'want/desire' closely tied to avowal and behavior; partially reformed alcoholics say that they have both a strong desire for drink and a desire that that desire not be gratified, and that these two conflict, and their behavior bears them out. Unregenerate alcoholics assert that they have a strong desire for drink and deny that they have any desire not to drink, and their behavior bears them out. Still, the unregenerate alcoholic has an interest in not drinking (and in developing the appropriate second-order desire) But what does it mean to say that alcoholics have an interest, but no desire to restrict their drinking other than that *we,* the outside observers, think that it would be better for them not to have the desire for drink? It would be no objection even if it meant no more than that, but confirmed alcoholics may share our judgment about their interests. They may agree that it is in their interest not to drink – they simply don't in fact have a desire which would make them act on this interest.

The concept of 'interest' is obscure partly because it is supposed to connect or 'mediate' 'reason' with the 'faculty of desire.'[4] Interests arise out of desires – I may have an interest in developing my lung capacity because I have a desire to play the flute better than I do – but that I have a desire doesn't by itself mean that I have the corresponding interest in bringing about conditions under which that desire will or can be satisfied; as the case of the alcoholic shows, I don't have that interest unless I have made some kind of judgment that the desire in question 'ought' to be satisfied, or that I have no overriding reason not to satisfy it. But recognition of interests may also give rise to new desires. Unregenerate alcoholics *have* no desire to stop drinking, but, if they recognize that it is in their interest to stop drinking, they may try to cultivate such a desire and may succeed, but it *is* in their interest to stop drinking whether they recognize it or not.

To speak of an agent's 'interests' is to speak of the way that agent's

4 EI 244ff [T1 198ff], esp. 250 [T1 201].

particular desires could be rationally integrated into a coherent 'good-life.'[5] Alcoholics can be said to have an 'interest' in giving up drink, even if they don't recognize it because we know that health (and, in extreme cases, life itself) is central to their conception of the 'good life' and that excessive drinking *cannot* be integrated into such a life.

Just as I may have wants and desires of which I am unaware – wants and desires I evince in my behavior, but which I do not recognize and avow – and needs of which I am unaware, I can also have interests of which I am unaware. From the fact that I have a certain need, it does not follow that I have a desire to satisfy that need. If I am unaware of the need I may not act in any way which could be construed as trying to satisfy the need.[6] However I do wish to say that I have an 'interest' in the satisfaction of anything which can reasonably be termed a 'need.'

There is no mystery, then, to the claim that agents are deceived or mistaken about their wants and desires or their interests. I may sincerely avow a desire which my behavior belies, or vehemently repudiate a desire, which, as my behavior shows, I clearly have. If the agents are unaware of some of their needs, they may have formed a set of interests which is incompatible with the satisfaction of those needs, or they may have formed a set of interests which is inconsistent or self-defeating, or I may have perfectly good 'empirical' grounds for thinking that the pursuit of their present set of interests will lead them not, as they suppose, to happiness, tranquility, and contentment, but to pain, misery, and frustration. If agents are deceived or mistaken about their interests, we will say that they are pursuing 'merely apparent' interests, and not their 'real' or 'true' interests.

What are the 'real' or 'true' or 'objective' interests of a group of agents, and how can they come to know them? I will distinguish two different approaches to the definition of the 'true' interests of a group: the 'perfect-knowledge approach,' and the 'optimal conditions' approach.

It is easy to see how the 'perfect-knowledge approach' might arise

---

[5] Certainly agents and groups don't strictly speaking *aim* at mere biological survival, but rather at the attainment of a 'good' life and at the reproduction of a particular cultural form of life. Cf. ZL 176ff, EI 350 [T1 288f], TW 162 [T1 312f], TG 146ff, WL 41 [T6 40f]. Note also the seventeenth-century usage of the term 'interest' reported by Hirschman (p. 32): 'it comprised the totality of human aspirations, but denoted an element of reflection or calculation with respect to the manner in which these aspirations were to be pursued.' In the limiting case – that of the alcoholic – the 'manner in which these aspirations were to be pursued' may be 'not at all.'

[6] There are, of course, many cases in which agents may systematically act to satisfy needs of which they never become aware. Some of the most interesting work in the social sciences is devoted to showing how social institutions are organized to achieve just this result. Harris (1974) is a good instance.

from a consideration of some of the examples we have discussed. If John is an unregenerate alcoholic, he has a first-order desire for drink and no second-order desire that that desire not be satisfied. We have said that this is compatible with John's recognizing that it is in his interest not to drink. He may recognize this and still not have the appropriate second-order desire, although the recognition itself may bring him to try to acquire or cultivate that desire. But, of course, John may *not* realize that it is in his interest to stop drinking. He may be very ignorant or have false views. He may think that drinking is good for his circulation, may never have heard of cirrhosis, etc. In that case we say that he is mistaken about his interests, and what we mean by that is that *if* he knew more than he does – if, for instance, he had correct views about the effect of his drinking on his health – he would recognize that it is not in his interest to continue to drink. By giving John the appropriate bits of knowledge we can bring him to a clearer and more correct view of his interests. From this is it but a step to the claim that John's 'real' or 'true' or 'objective' interests are the ones he would have in the limiting case in which he had 'perfect' knowledge.

What does this 'perfect knowledge' comprise? Presumably it must include at least all empirical knowledge of the kind that can be provided by the sciences, but does it include such things as the kind of self-knowledge acquired in psychoanalysis, or knowledge of what would satisfy me? Do I know my real interests if I have available 'perfect' empirical knowledge, but have not used it to reflect correctly on my present wants and interests so as to make them consistent? If the Marquis de Sade had had the final Intergalactic edition of the Encyclopaedia Britannica at his disposal would what he pursued then have been his 'true' interests?

The 'optimal conditions' approach starts from the observation that the desires and hence the interests of human agents have been extremely variable, and that what desires and interests the agents will form will depend to a large extent on the circumstances in which they find themselves. In particular, we are familiar with cases in which agents in circumstances of extreme deprivation develop pathological desires and interests. Thus, the Ik, who live in the border area between Uganda, Kenya, and the Sudan are said to recognize a full stomach as the only good – they routinely steal food from the very young, the old, and the infirm, leaving them to die – and their chief joy in life seems to be Schadenfreude.[7] The anthropologist who first described this tribe thinks that this value system is a response to a couple of generations of

[7] Turnbull (1972).

famine, but that the value system is now 'stable' and does not change
even when the food supply improves,

for it was obvious from the outset that nothing had really changed due to the
sudden glut of food, except to cause interpersonal relationships to deteriorate
still further if possible, and heighten Icien individualism beyond what I would
have thought even the Ik to be capable of. If they had been mean and greedy
and selfish before with nothing to be mean and greedy and selfish over, now that
they had something they really excelled themselves in what would be an insult
to animals to call bestiality.[8]

This value system is an understandable, and even in some sense 'rational' adaptation to the horrifying conditions in which the Ik live, but
do we wish to say that the Ik are pursuing their 'true' or 'real' interests
when they engage in their typically spiteful behavior, cultivate duplicity,
train themselves to feel as little connection with or sympathy for others
as possible, take delight in tormenting the old and feeble members of
the group, ridicule those who show signs of residual altruism, etc.? We
can say that they are not acting on their true interests because we think
that we have grounds for the belief that they would *not* have formed
these desires and interests had they not been living in objectively horrifying conditions. The desires and interests are pathological because
the conditions in which they were formed are horrible. The 'optimal
conditions' approach attempts to turn this intuition around and say that
the agents' 'real' interests are the interests they would have formed in
'optimal' (i.e. beneficent) conditions. But what are the 'optimal conditions' for forming interests? It is easier to say what conditions clearly
are not optimal, that is, which are positive hindrances to the formation
of 'true' interests, than to specify which conditions are optimal. Agents
are unlikely to form their interests 'correctly' in conditions of extreme
physical deprivation, in circumstances where they are maltreated or un-
duly coerced, pressured, or influenced, or in conditions of gross ignorance or false belief.

Prima facie, the two senses of 'real interests' would seem to be quite
distinct. The interests these particular agents with this particular initial
form of consciousness in these specific objective circumstances would
form if they had perfect knowledge need not be the interests they
would form if they had been able to form their wants and interests in
optimal conditions. To put the same thing another way, the task of
becoming fully aware of the wants and interests one *actually* has is different from the task of acquiring the 'right' human interests – the ones
one would have been able to acquire had one lived in supremely fortu-

---

[8] Turnbull, p. 280.

nate circumstances. The first of these two tasks is very much like that of working out the 'ideology' of a group in the positive sense,[9] i.e. elaborating the set of beliefs, wants, and interests most appropriate to the agents' real situation and given initial form of consciousness.[10]

The difference between the two senses of 'real interests' is particularly clear in the example of the Ik. Give the Ik *any* amount of further empirical knowledge and any amount of 'self-knowledge,' i.e. reflective awareness of their own wants, and the chances are that as long as they remain in their present situation, they will at best develop more sophisticated versions of their present pathological form of consciousness.

This appearance of divergence between the two senses of 'real interests' might, however, be deceptive. It is easy to see how someone could argue that 'optimal conditions' must include not merely the absence of gross ignorance and false belief, but 'perfect knowledge.' Still the Ik-example would seem to stand against any complete identification of 'real interests' in the two senses. But does it?

We are granting that if the Ik were to acquire perfect knowledge of the world, their situation, and themselves, they would probably form a set of interests which we would characterize as revolting and pathological – partly this is because the objective situation of the Ik is appalling, and partly because the Ik were rather disgusting characters to start with. We were further claiming that the interests the Ik would form if they had perfect knowledge would not be their 'true' or 'real' interests because they would not be identical with the interests they would form under optimal conditions. But what real grounds do we have for denying that these would be the Ik's 'true' interests? That *we* don't find them attractive is no argument. It is agreed that this is what they would come up with if they had perfect knowledge, it is even granted that these revolting interests are in some way appropriate for survival in the difficult circumstances in which the Ik must live. What more can one ask?

Those who would argue that the interests the Ik would form under conditions of perfect knowledge needn't be their 'true interests' may be motivated by the assumption that the 'real' or 'true' interests of any human group can't be ones of which we would strongly disapprove ethically. The 'real' interests need not be ones we would ourselves adopt or

---

[9] Vide supra, pp. 22–6.
[10] It is tempting to associate the first of these two senses of 'real interest' with the psychoanalytic model – reflective self-knowledge is to help individual agents realize their true interests – and the second with Marxist social theory – a systematic view of how the wants and interests of human groups are formed (and deformed) under varying socio-economic circumstances.

share – we can be pluralists about that – but they must not be morally unacceptable. The implication is that if one enforces the requirement that the 'real interests' are those the agents would acquire under optimal conditions, this will insure that they are morally acceptable.

'Real interests' are a topic of discussion here because an ideology is supposed to be a kind of mistake agents make about their real interests (from which Ideologiekritik can free them). But the Ik, as far as we can tell, are not ideologically deluded; their problem is that they are starving to death. That we morally disapprove of the form of consciousness the Ik have, and would disapprove of the interests they would form were they to have perfect knowledge, is irrelevant to the task of Ideologiekritik and to the notion of 'real interests' associated with it. Ideologiekritik is supposed to have moral implications, but it isn't a form of moralizing criticism, and doesn't *start* from ethical assumptions. Ideologiekritik is supposed to enlighten the agents about their true interests by freeing them from errors and delusions about their real situation in the world. There may be other senses of 'real interests,' but they are irrelevant to Ideologiekritik; 'real interests' for Ideologiekritik are those the agents would form, if they had perfect knowledge.

But are our only grounds for objecting to the 'real interests' the Ik would form if they had perfect knowledge our own distaste and moral disapprobation? Certainly, that their objective circumstances are horrifying is not *just* a judgment we, as outside observers, make. We have reason to believe that the Ik even now realize that their objective situation is dismal, and that they would prefer not to live as they do. If the Ik would prefer not to *live* in their present state of extreme malnutrition, presumably they would also prefer not to have to form their desires and interests in such circumstances. Now if the Ik are assumed to have 'perfect knowledge' part of what they will know is what the 'optimal conditions' for forming desires and interests are. These conditions, the reader will recall, are conditions of non-deprivation, non-coercion, and minimally correct information. With perfect knowledge, the Ik will know what interests *they* would form if they were to live in 'optimal conditions,' and we may safely assume that they would *prefer* to live in 'optimal conditions.' Can we, then, still assume that, if in possession of perfect knowledge, the Ik will acquire only a more sophisticated version of their present bestial form of consciousness?

If the answer to this question is a clear and resounding 'yes,' we can predict how the argument will run: To be sure, if the conditions of existence for the Ik were radically different from what they are, the Ik would have a very different set of interests – they themselves realize that – but from that it in no way follows that the interests they *would* have in some totally different situation are their present true or 'real' interests. The Ik may yearn to live in radically altered circumstances and speculate on what they would desire in such a case, but such vague yearning and such utopian speculation are vain and ineffective, and have nothing to do with their interests in the real world; look at how they actually act when they have perfect knowledge.

Recall, however, the case of the unreformed alcoholics; they have no effective desire to stop drinking, but the sheer fact that they could recognize that it would be in their interest to stop drinking was considered grounds enough for attributing this interest to them; 'interests' are related not only to (effective) desire, but also to judgment. Similarly, if the Ik recognize – as we assume they do – that there is another set of interests they would prefer to have, namely the ones they realize they would acquire in the circumstances in which they would prefer to live, then those interests *are* their real interests (and not the sophisticated but bestial ones we see them actually pursue). The Iks' perception that under optimal conditions they would have interests very different from those they have now is unlikely under present circumstances to be very effective in changing their hideous form of consciousness, but that doesn't imply that the interests they know that they would have under optimal conditions are not their 'real' interests. Alcoholics' perception that it is not in their interest to drink is often not very effective either.

This example does suggest a convergence of the two senses of 'real interests.' If the agents have the requisite 'perfect knowledge' the interests they will acknowledge as their 'real interests' will be those they know they would form under optimal conditions of non-deprivation and non-coercion.

This conclusion is one the members of the Frankfurt School would probably wish to defend, but for slightly different reasons. To speak of 'perfect knowledge' is already to enter the realm of science fiction, but in the case of the Ik we can be quite sure that their lives are so impoverished, stultified, and constricted that they will never get anywhere near 'perfect knowledge' of themselves and of their natural and social environment. A society *all* of whose members have been on the verge of starvation for decades is unlikely to develop sophisticated forms of knowledge. To acquire knowledge requires not just a minimal economic surplus but an ability to experiment, to try out alternatives, a kind of freedom to experience and discuss the results of experience.

Certainly the 'self-knowledge' the members of the Frankfurt School have in mind as part of 'perfect knowledge' – knowledge of one's own wants, needs, motives, of what kind of life one would find acceptable and satisfying – is something agents are very unlikely to attain in a society without extensive room for free discussion and the unrestrained play of the imagination with alternative ways of living. None of this is possible in a society as impoverished, constricted, and oppressive as that of the Ik. The Iks' motivation is transparent: Grab as much food as possible and avoid all unnecessary exertion. In such circumstances discussion of wants, motives, etc. is totally pointless. Like agents in an ideally free society – inhabitants of 'utopia' – the Ik have completely transparent motivation, but they don't have a high level of self-knowledge. They don't have knowledge of their own human possibilities and can't see their form of life against a background of envisaged alternatives.

This line of argument shows how 'real interests' in both senses might converge, but only at the cost of creating a double bind: the interests the agents would form given perfect knowledge coincide with those they would form in optimal conditions, because the agents couldn't acquire 'perfect knowledge' unless they were in 'optimal conditions.' But to be in 'optimal conditions' is not only to be in conditions of freedom, but also not to lack any relevant knowledge. We can't be fully free without having perfect knowledge, nor acquire perfect knowledge unless we live in conditions of complete freedom. Our 'real interests' are those we would form in such conditions of perfect knowledge and freedom. Although we can be in a position fully to recognize our 'real interests' only if our society satisfies the utopian condition of perfect freedom, still, although we do not live in that utopia, we may be free enough to recognize how we might act to abolish some of the coercion from which we suffer and move closer to 'optimal conditions' of freedom and knowledge. The task of a critical theory is to show us which way to move.

3

CRITICAL THEORY

1 COGNITIVE STRUCTURE

The members of the Frankfurt School distinguish sharply between scientific theories and critical theories.[1] These two kinds of theory are said to differ along three important dimensions.

First, they differ in their aim or goal, and hence in the way agents can use or apply them. Scientific theories have as their aim or goal successful manipulation of the external world; they have 'instrumental use.' If correct, they enable the agents who have mastered them to cope effectively with the environment and thus pursue their chosen ends successfully. Critical theories aim at emancipation and enlightenment, at making agents aware of hidden coercion, thereby freeing them from that coercion and putting them in a position to determine where their true interests lie.

Second, critical and scientific theories differ in their 'logical' or 'cognitive' structure. Scientific theories are 'objectifying.' That means that at least in typical cases one can distinguish clearly between the theory and the 'objects' to which the theory refers; the theory isn't itself part of the object-domain it describes. Newton's theory isn't itself a particle in motion. Critical theories, on the other hand, are claimed to be 'reflective,' or 'self-referential': a critical theory is itself always a part of the object-domain which it describes; critical theories are always in part about themselves.

Finally, critical and scientific theories differ in the kind of evidence which would be relevant for determining whether or not they are cognitively acceptable, that is, they admit of and require different kinds of confirmation. Scientific theories require empirical confirmation through observation and experiment; critical theories are cognitively acceptable only if they survive a more complicated process of evalua-

---

[1] Habermas, under the influence of Gadamer, adds 'interpretations' as yet a third separate kind of 'theory.' Just as the goal of science is to develop scientific theories, so the goal of philology is to provide 'interpretations' of texts (TW 155ff [T1 308ff]).

tion, the central part of which is a demonstration that they are 'reflectively acceptable.'

In this section and those that follow I will try to clarify the claim that critical theories have a distinctive aim or use, a distinctive cognitive structure, and a distinctive mode of confirmation.

Any society at any time will be characterized by a certain distribution of beliefs among its members. This distribution will include beliefs about the structure, institutions, and present state of the society. There is nothing wrong with describing this state of affairs on analogy with the case of an individual human subject as one in which the society 'reflects' on itself or has 'reflective beliefs' about itself, as long as it is clear that what is meant is just a distribution of many, possibly very different beliefs among the various members of the society. Social theory is continuous with the 'naive' beliefs agents have about their society. Any social theory is a set of beliefs some agent – at least the social theorist who propounds it – has about society, so it, too, can be described as a way in which the society 'reflects on itself.'

It is an essential task of any complete theory of society to investigate not just social institutions and practices, but also the beliefs agents have about their society – to investigate not just 'social reality' in the narrowest sense, but also the 'social knowledge' which is part of that reality. A full-scale social theory, then, will form part of its own object-domain. That is, a social theory is a theory *about* (among other things) agents' beliefs about their society, but it is *itself* such a belief. So if a theory of society is to give an exhaustive account of the beliefs agents in the society have, it will have to give an account of itself as one such belief.

A social theory is said to have a 'reflective cognitive structure' if it gives an explicit account of its own 'context of origin and context of application.'[2] Thus, the Marxist theory of society is a full-scale social theory in that it purports to give an account both of the 'objective' social and economic institutions of the society and of the major kinds of beliefs the agents in the society hold. It has an explicitly reflective cognitive structure in that:

(a) it contains an account of its own genesis and origin, i.e. it purports to explain how it came about that mid-nineteenth-century European capitalist society was able to develop the correct knowledge of itself embodied in Marxism. Marxism purports to explain how it was possible for Marxism to arise when and where it did;

(b) it 'anticipates' its own use or application by members of the society.

[2] TP 9f, 17 [T4 1f, 10]; KK 392f.

Those of us brought up on one of those views of the nature of science which stress the structural identity of explanation and prediction may be sorely tempted to take the above the wrong way. We may be tempted to take it to mean that Marxism is a theory with great explanatory and predictive power. It can even explain its own origin – that is (a) above – and can predict that it will be used by members of the society (the proletariat) to effect certain social changes – that is (b) above. It might be thought that this is enough to distinguish a critical theory from a scientific theory. Although scientific theories may be used to predict natural events like eclipses, or to predict what will occur *if* agents decide to use these theories in certain ways, they can't in general be used to predict whether or not the agents will decide to use them.

However this might be, 'anticipate' does not mean 'predict' for Habermas. This is clear from his essay on Benjamin[3] in which he contrasts the attitude of Benjamin on the end of 'bourgeois art' with that of Marcuse. Benjamin is said to have 'described' the process by which art lost its aura; Marcuse, on the other hand, is said to have 'anticipated' the same development. 'Anticipation' is then glossed as 'Forderung' ('demand' or 'requirement').[4] Marcuse doesn't *predict* that 'bourgeois art' will end; he shows that it is a demand or requirement of rationality that it end.

A critical theory, then, does not predict *that* the agents in the society will adopt and use the theory to understand themselves and transform their society, rather it 'demands' that they adopt the critical theory, i.e. it asserts that these agents 'ought' to adopt and act on the critical theory where the 'ought' is the 'ought' of rationality. From the fact that it would be rational for the agents in the society to adopt the critical theory, it doesn't follow that one can predict that they will adopt it.[5]

Scientific theories don't 'anticipate' their own use in this technical sense of 'anticipate.' Even if it is rational for agents to use them, scientific theories don't themselves contain assertions to that effect. No scientific theory states of itself that agents ought to adopt it for use. Furthermore, although the members of the Frankfurt School assume that scientific theories are always in principle transformable into technologies which would make them guides to effective human action,[6] they also think that it is never more than conditionally rational for human

---

[3] 'Bewußtmachende oder rettende Kritik – Die Aktualität Walter Benjamins' in KK 302ff.
[4] KK 309, 312.
[5] Although a critical theory might and in general will contain as a part of itself an empirical theory of the society which might allow a prediction of this type. It is not in virtue of this kind of prediction that the whole theory is a *critical* theory.
[6] N2 400, TP 26f [T4 19f].

agents to adopt a given scientific technology. A technology gives agents means for bringing about states of affairs of some specified sort. *If* I have an interest in states of affairs of this type, then it is rational for me to make use of the technology. But I may have no such interest, and there will be nothing in the scientific theory on which the technology is based to assert that I *ought* to have this interest or that this interest is a rational one for me to have. If the technology deals with matters irrelevant to my concerns, it is not rational for me to adopt it, and the scientific theory on which it is based should equally become a matter of indifference to me.

A critical theory, on the other hand, asserts of itself that it is not a matter of indifference to some group of agents. It doesn't merely give information about how it would be rational for agents to act *if* they had certain interests; it claims to inform them about what interests it is rational for them to have.

The *effect* of a successful critical theory is supposed to be emancipation and enlightenment. To be more exact, a critical theory has as its inherent aim to be the self-consciousness of a successful process of enlightenment and emancipation.[7] Ignoring for the moment the odd clause to the effect that the theory must be the 'self-consciousness' of the process, what is meant by 'emancipation and enlightenment?' Various texts inform us that 'emancipation and enlightenment' refer to a social transition from an initial state to a final state which has the following properties:

(a) The initial state is one *both* of false consciousness and error, *and* of 'unfree existence.'[8]
(b) In the initial state false consciousness and unfree existence are inherently connected so that agents can be liberated from one only if they are also at the same time freed from the other.[9]
(c) The 'unfree existence' from which the agents in the initial state suffer is a form of *self-imposed* coercion; their false consciousness is a kind of *self-delusion*.[10]
(d) The coercion from which the agents suffer in the initial state is one whose 'power'[11] or 'objectivity'[12] derives *only* from the fact that the agents do not realize that it is self-imposed.
(e) The final state is one in which the agents are free of false consciousness – they have been enlightened – and free of self-imposed coercion – they have been emancipated.

[7] Cf. WL 7, 9 [T6 9, 11]; PS 191, 261 [T3 162, 221].
[8] EI 256, 348f [T1 208, 286f], TP 16f [T4 9f].
[9] TP 315 [T4 262], EI 362f [T1 298f].
[10] N2 412, 400ff.   [11] EI 348 [T1 286].   [12] TP 307 [T4 253f].

Following this schema I will first try to describe in more detail the initial state of bondage and delusion from which the agents are to be freed; then I will try to describe the process by which they are enlightened and emancipated.

Societies which have reached a certain level of organisational complexity – certainly all societies organized as 'states' – have institutional mechanisms for reaching decisions about collective action. People in healthy, well-functioning societies usually accept[13] even those social decisions which manifestly thwart their own immediate, perceived wants and preferences, provided they believe that these decisions are legitimate.[14] Agents will take *individual* decisions to be legitimate if:

(a) they assume them to be 'formally' or 'procedurally' correct, i.e. if they assume that the basic decision-making institutions have operated in their accustomed way, according to their acknowledged rules of procedure to produce this decision;
(b) they assume that the basic decision-making institutions (and the rules under which they operate) are legitimate.[15]

To say that the members of the society take a basic social institution to be 'legitimate' is to say that they take it to 'follow' from a system of norms they all accept; agents think the norm-system capable of conferring legitimacy because they accept a set of general beliefs (normative beliefs and other kinds of beliefs) which are organized into a world-picture which they assume all members of the society hold. So a social institution is considered legitimate if it can be shown to stand in the right relation to the basic world-picture of the group. A social institution or practice can be extremely repressive – it may thwart and frustrate the agents in the pursuit of many of their strongest desires – and still be accepted by the members of the society because they take it to be legitimate, and they take it to be legitimate because of certain normative beliefs deeply embedded in their world-picture.

Suppose now that the world picture of a group is ideologically false and is used to legitimize an extremely repressive set of basic social institutions. Suppose further that the reason the agents hold this ideologi-

---

[13] What does it mean to say that the agents generally 'accept' decisions? That they march out of the Ekklesia whistling the paean? That their level of acquiescence or merely passive resistance is such that normal governmental operations can continue (without mobilization of the National Guard)?

[14] TG 120, 244, 247; note esp. the phrase 'auch gegen das Interesse der Betroffenen' at TG 244.

[15] TG 265ff.

cally false world-picture is that they live in a society with these particular coercive social institutions. If the basic social institutions are very coercive, one result may be that the very structure of communication in the society becomes 'distorted,' but if the basic structure of communication in the society is distorted the world-picture may never come up for free discussion, and hence may be immunized from criticism.[16]

In this situation conditions (a) and (b) of the scheme[17] are satisfied. The agents are suffering from false consciousness – their world-picture is ideologically false – and their 'existence' is 'unfree' – their basic social institutions are extremely coercive. Further there is an inherent connection between the false consciousness and the 'unfree existence'; agents can't be freed from one without also being freed from the other. They can't be freed from their coercive social institutions as long as they retain the ideological world-picture which legitimizes them, nor can they get rid of their ideological world-picture as long as their basic coercive social institutions render it immune to free discussion and criticism.

It is also not hard to see in what sense the 'unfree existence' from which the agents suffer is a form of *self-imposed* coercion. Social institutions are not natural phenomena; they don't just exist of and by themselves. The agents in a society impose coercive institutions on themselves by participating in them, accepting them without protest, etc. Simply by acting in an apparently 'free' way according to the dictates of their world-picture, the agents reproduce relations of coercion.

In holding their false form of consciousness, their ideological world-picture, the agents in the society are deluding themselves. Ideological error isn't a mistake the agents make for some accidental reason (like a mistake in long division due to lapse of attention), nor does someone *else* (consciously) deceive the agents (the priests haven't formed a conspiracy and succeeded in putting one over on us). In acting, the agents 'produce' their basic social institutions, and it is the normal operation of these social institutions which maintains the world-picture. The 'illusion' embodied in that world-picture is the result of the agents' own activity reacting on them.

Once the agents are *in* this situation, how can they ever get out of it? In what sense is their world-picture ideologically false and how can they ever come to realize that it is? How can a transition from this initial state of self-reinforcing bondage and delusion to a final state of enlightenment and emancipation ever take place?

The usual answer is that agents are enlightened and emancipated by

[16] LS 34 [T2 19], TG 258f, 246f, TP 19 [T4 11f].
[17] Vide supra p. 58.

a critical theory. The critical theory induces self-reflection in the agents; by reflecting they come to realize that their form of consciousness is ideologically false and that the coercion from which they suffer is self-imposed. But, by (d) of the schema, once they have realized this, the coercion loses its 'power' or 'objectivity' and the agents are emancipated.[18]

What is this 'self-reflection?' What does it do? How does it work? In Habermas' various writings one can find three kinds of statements about 'self-reflection':

1. Self-reflection 'dissolves' a) 'self-generated objectivity,' and b) 'objective illusion'.[19]
2. Self-reflection makes the subject aware of its own genesis or origin.[20]
3. Self-reflection operates by bringing to consciousness unconscious determinants of action, or consciousness.[21]

So it seems that a critical theory shows agents that their form of consciousness (or world-picture) is ideologically false by making them aware of some unconscious determinants of that form of consciousness. But why should this be sufficient to convince the agents that they are suffering from ideological delusion? Agents don't *generally* come to think that their beliefs are false if they discover that they have been 'determined' by factors of which they were unaware.

Consider the following picture of the human cognitive subject: Human agents don't merely have and acquire beliefs, they also have ways of criticizing and evaluating their own beliefs. Every agent will have a set of epistemic principles, i.e. an at least rudimentary set of second-order beliefs about such things as what kinds of beliefs are acceptable or unacceptable, and how beliefs can be shown to be acceptable or unacceptable. Agents will often share their epistemic principles with the other members of their social group, and, just as agents will have views about what are good and what bad conditions for forming wants and interests, they may also have views about what are good and what bad conditions for forming and acquiring beliefs of various sorts. If they have such views, we will want to count them as belonging to the set of the agents' epistemic principles, too.

In particular, agents may think that *some* conditions for forming beliefs of a particular kind are not merely unpromising, but positively

---

[18] Vide supra p. 58.
[19] N2 400f, 412f, EI 362f [T1 298f], TG 246f. On the notion of 'objective illusion' vide infra pp. 70ff.
[20] TG 230f, EI 27, 29f, 317, etc. [T1 17f, 19, 260].
[21] N2 412f, TP 29 [T4 22f].

pernicious, so that any belief which could *only* have been acquired under those particularly unpropitious conditions is *ipso facto* unacceptable.

With this picture in mind, then, we may call a belief 'reflectively unacceptable' to a group of agents if they would give it up, were they to reflect on it in the light of information about the conditions under which they could have acquired it. Suppose now that the agents in a society have a set of epistemic principles with the following provision for evaluating those beliefs which are to serve as sources of legitimation in the society: Legitimizing beliefs are acceptable *only* if they *could* have been acquired by the agents in a free and uncoerced discussion in which all members of the society take part.[22]

If the agents have this kind of normative epistemology, Ideologiekritik can operate. Their world-picture is the ultimate source of legitimation in society, however it would not be found acceptable in free discussion; the agents continue to hold it because their coercive social institutions prevent them from ever subjecting the world-picture to free discussion. Ideologiekritik shows the agents that this world-picture is *false* consciousness by showing them that it is reflectively unacceptable to them, i.e. by showing them that they could have acquired it *only* under conditions of coercion.

It is obvious that the notion of a set of epistemic principles must bear a lot of weight in this argument. But how do we pick out epistemic principles – after all, they may be held merely tacitly – and how do we know when we have described them correctly? Is there always just one well-defined set of epistemic principles to each well-defined human social group? (This seems unlikely.) How would we know? Will the epistemic principles used by agents simply vary from human group to human group, and from epoch to epoch? Or are there some invariant or universal features all such sets of epistemic principles share? Are sets of epistemic principles just historical givens which it makes no sense even to try to compare or evaluate, or is there some standard by reference to which we might be able to conclude that one is 'better' than another? For that matter, can just *any* collection of principles for evaluating and accepting or rejecting beliefs count as a set of *epistemic* principles? By what right is a principle for evaluating legitimizing beliefs in the society an epistemic principle?

The answers given to these questions will have wide-reaching implications for the status of Ideologiekritik and of the critical theory. The agents' epistemic principles are of central importance for the critical enterprise; the critical theory shows that a form of consciousnes or

[22] Vide LS 125, 148.

world-picture is false by showing that it is reflectively unacceptable to the agents, *given their epistemic principles*.

Among the proponents of the critical theory one can find two quite different views about reflection and the standing of epistemic principles. The first of these two views I will associate with Adorno.[23] Adorno was the most consistent proponent of a contextualist or historicist approach to reflection in general and to the criticism of ideology in particular. Agents' epistemic principles and their standards of reflective acceptability just vary historically. Our standards of reflective acceptability and the social and cultural ideals in terms of which we criticize societies and ideologies are just part of our tradition and have no absolute foundation or transcendental warrant. For Adorno we must start from where we happen to be historically and culturally, from a particular kind of frustration or suffering experienced by human agents in their attempt to realize some historically specific project of 'the good life.' The critical theories we propound in the course of this undertaking are extraordinarily fragile historical entities, which, even if effective and 'true,' can never lay claim to any absolute standing — they are effective and 'true' only relative to this particular historical situation and are bound to be superseded.

This contextualist view of Adorno's fits in well with the strongly held Frankfurt view that a critical theory is 'directed at' or 'addressed to' a particular group of human agents and contributes in a special way to their self-knowledge.[24] A critical theory helps the members of the group to self-knowledge by making explicit for them the epistemic principles they already use (but of which they are not perhaps fully aware) and by giving them knowledge of the implications of these epistemic principles for the rest of their beliefs, i.e. a critical theory gives them knowledge of what changes would result if they were to apply the standards of rationality they tacitly accept in a consistent and thoroughgoing way to the whole body of their beliefs. A critical theory is addressed to the members of *this* particular social group in the sense that it describes *their* epistemic principles and *their* ideal of the 'good life' and demonstrates that some belief they hold is reflectively unacceptable for agents who hold their epistemic principles and a source of frustration for agents who are trying to realize this particular kind of 'good life.' In general, then, a critical theory specifies for *these* agents how they would have to modify their beliefs to attain *their* ideal of a rational, satisfying existence.

---

[23] Vide Habermas' essay on Adorno 'Urgeschichte der Subjektivität und verwilderte Selbstbehauptung' in PP.

[24] Cf. TP 9f, 29f, 37f [T4 1f, 22f, 32].

The second of the two views on reflection to be found among the
members of the Frankfurt School is one I will associate with the later
Habermas. In some of his earliest essays Habermas follows Adorno and
holds a contextualist view of reflection; then, sometime in the mid
1960s, he seems to have been frightened by the specter of relativism,
and retreated into a kind of transcendentalism.[25] The assumption on
which the whole critical enterprise rests is that the agents to whom the
critical theory is addressed are ideologically deluded, i.e. that they are
suffering from false consciousness. The way in which they are to be
freed from this false consciousness is by being brought to realize that
parts of their form of consciousness are reflectively unacceptable. The
argument for reflective unacceptability, however, depends on an appeal
to the agents' epistemic principles, but, if the agents' epistemic principles are themselves just part of their traditional form of consciousness,
how can we know that they are not themselves 'ideologically
distorted?'[26] The more deeply seated the agents' false consciousness,
the more they need emancipation, but also the more likely it is that
their epistemic principles will be part of their problem and not part of
a solution. Thus, according to Habermas, a part of a form of consciousness is reflectively unacceptable if it could not have been acquired by
the agents except under conditions of coercion. But if the society in
which they live is extraordinarily coercive and their form of consciousness very 'distorted,' why should we assume that their beliefs about what
count as 'conditions of coercion' will remain immune from ideological
distortion? But if the agents have radically 'wrong' views about what
counts as coercion and what as freedom or autonomy, then to throw
out all the parts of their form of consciousness which they could only
have acquired under *what they take* to be coercion may well result in
driving them yet deeper into delusion.

The contextualist response to the considerations of the previous paragraph is that if there is a problem here it is a problem with life and not
a problem with the critical theory. Critical theory is committed to the
principle of 'internal criticism.' Just as a critical theory is supposed to

[25] For Habermas' early position vide TP 303f and also footnote 25 p. 306 added in the
second edition in which Habermas withdraws the claim in the main text. [This essay is not
included in the English translation T4.] When Habermas claims in PS 254 [T3 214f] that
'critique' cannot be defined, I take this as a sign of contextualism; the theory of the 'ideal
speech situation' he develops in his later transcendentalist mood is precisely an attempt to
define 'critique.' The single most important document in this context is Habermas' paper
on Adorno 'Urgeschichte der Subjektivität und verwilderte Selbstbehauptung' in PP
184ff.

[26] This consideration is urged against Habermas' early position by H. Pilot in his paper
'Jürgen Habermas' empirisch falsifizierbare Geschichtsphilosophie' in PS 307ff [T3
258ff].

contribute to the agents' self-knowledge, so the proponents of the critical theory recognize as 'valid criticism' only what could in principle be part of the self-criticism of the agents to whom it is addressed; if the proponents of a critical theory wish to enlighten and emancipate a group of agents, they must find in the experience, form of consciousness, and belief of *those* agents the means of emancipation and enlightenment. If we can't find the appropriate experiences of suffering and frustration and the appropriate principles of reflective acceptability in the life and form of consciousness of those agents, Ideologiekritik cannot begin, and we have no right to call the agents 'deluded.' We may be quite revolted by their mode of life, but we have no apriori or transcendental guarantee that either they or we will ultimately turn out to have been deluded and that in their case or in our case Ideologiekritik will have had room to operate.

Habermas rejects this contextualist view. He thinks that he can give something like a transcendental argument to the conclusion that *all* agents must agree in finding reflectively unacceptable any part of their form of consciousness which could only have been acquired under conditions of coercion. He further thinks that he can show that *all* agents have a tacit commitment to the *same* views about what conditions are coercive.

The starting point of Habermas' 'transcendental argument' is a set of views about language-use and its preconditions.[27] To be a human agent, he argues, is to participate at least potentially in a speech community, and to be something *we* can recognize as a human agent means to participate at least potentially in *our* speech community. But no agent can be even potentially a member of a speech community who cannot recognize the difference between true and false statements in some general way or who doesn't in some way know what it means for a statement to be true.[28] But what it means for a statement to be true is that it would be the one on which all agents would agree if they were to discuss all of human experience in absolutely free and uncoerced circumstances for an indefinite period of time. So anyone we recognize as a human agent will thereby stand committed to agreeing with us on what to count as conditions of 'free and uncoerced discussion,' and hence must in some way share our views on what are conditions of freedom and what conditions of coercion. Habermas uses the term 'ideal speech situation' to refer to a situation of absolutely uncoerced and unlimited discussion between completely free and equal human agents.[29]

[27] TG 101ff. gives the clearest exposition of this part of his theory.
[28] TG 113f, 135.
[29] WT 252ff, TG 135ff.

The 'ideal speech situation' will serve Habermas as a transcendental criterion of truth, freedom, and rationality.[30] Beliefs agents would agree on in the ideal speech situation are *ipso facto* 'true beliefs,' preferences they would agree on are 'rational preferences,' interests they would agree on are 'real interests.' The agents are 'free' if their real situation is one which satisfies the conditions of the 'ideal speech situation.'

Habermas claims that *all* human agents in *every* action they perform (and, in particular, in every speech act) must 'presuppose' the ideal speech situation, or 'assume it counterfactually,' that is, they must 'act as if' their present situation *was* 'ideal,' although they can never *know* that it is and will generally have reason to believe that it is not.[31] In Habermas' technical jargon, agents are said to 'anticipate' the ideal speech situation whenever they act, that is, in acting they are said to commit themselves to using acceptability in the ideal speech situation as criterion of truth (for proposition) and of 'moral' acceptability (for norms). This means, in particular, that agents are committed to accepting as valid any criticism of their action which shows that action to be based on norms which would not be freely agreed on in the ideal speech situation.

Agents obviously couldn't use acceptability in the ideal speech situation as a criterion of truth if they didn't know what an ideal speech situation was, and couldn't tell at all what features such an ideal speech situation would have. So every human agent must have an innate capacity to 'construct' the ideal speech situation, i.e. given the proper conditions, and perhaps proper guidance and prompting, any agent should be able to recognize what features an ideal speech situation would have.

Even if one grants that to be a human agent implies to be able to make some distinction between 'true' and 'false,' it doesn't follow that to be a human agent one must hold Habermas' 'consensus theory of truth,' i.e. the view that truth consists in consensus in the ideal speech situation. I find it quite hard to burden pre-dynastic Egyptians, ninth-century French serfs and early-twentieth-century Yanomamö tribesmen with the view that they are acting correctly if their action is based on a norm on which there would be universal consensus in an ideal speech situation. The notion that social institutions should be based on the free consent of those affected is a rather recent Western invention, but one which is now widely held. The notions that an action is morally acceptable or a belief 'true' if they would be the object of universal consensus under ideal conditions is an even more recent invention held

[30] TG 139, 224.
[31] TG 122, 128, 136, 140; WT 258f.

perhaps by a couple of professional philosophers in Germany and the United States. Appeal to the example of Chomsky here seems to me quite misguided.[32] Not all speakers of a language are aware of or could formulate a correct generative grammar of that language, but tacit knowledge of the rules of the generative grammar is posited to explain agents' intuitions of grammaticality. We have grounds for attributing the knowledge of this grammar to the agents if the grammar correctly predicts which statements the agents will accept as grammatical and which they will reject as ungrammatical. The point is not that pre-dynastic Egyptians couldn't formulate the 'consensus theory of truth,' but that we have no reason to think that they had any inclination to accept as legitimate only those social institutions on which they thought there would be universal consensus in ideal conditions. Furthermore, is it really plausible to think that we and they would agree on what counts as coercion and what as freedom? Habermas seems to be engaged in giving a transcendental deduction of a series of non facts.

Habermas' 'contextualist' opponents are, of course, free to adopt practically the whole of his substantive analysis, as long as they reject the transcendentalist underpinnings. To be sure, *our* real interests *are* the ones we would form in conditions of complete freedom of discussion, and any beliefs we could have acquired only under conditions of coercion we *will* find unacceptable, but these are just facts about us and our form of consciousness, just complex results of our particular history and traditions, and of no transcendental standing.

Habermas shows a sporadic awareness of some of these problems in occasional remarks about the history of forms of social legitimation.[33] He seems to distinguish several historical stages:

(a) an archaic stage in which agents use particular myths to give a narrative account of their social world and institutions;[34]

(b) a 'traditional' stage in which agents use unified mythic, religious, or metaphysical world-pictures or views about reality as a whole to legitimize their social institutions. Although these world-pictures are not just sequences of narratives, but are 'argumentatively structured,' they aren't themselves ever called into question and needn't ever prove their own validity as sources of legitimation;[35]

(c) a 'modern' stage characterised by the appearance of 'ideologies in the narrow sense.' These ideologies claim to be 'scientific,' i.e. to be able to give a full argumentative account of themselves and legiti-

[32] TG 101.
[33] Vide esp. ZR 329f.
[34] ZR 18f, 97.
[35] TW 65f [T5 94f], LS 33f [T2 18f].

mate the social order by appeal to universal norms and principles, universalizable interests, and interpretations of the 'good life.'[36]

(d) (purportedly) 'post-ideological' forms of social legitimation which claim to justify the social order by exclusive reference to its technical efficiency and which reject any appeal to moral principles, norms, or ideals of the 'good life' as 'ideological' (in the pejorative sense).[37]

If one looks closely at the characteristics implicitly attributed to agents in 'archaic societies' – they don't yet even *claim* to give *arguments* for their social arrangements, they are satisfied with particular narratives; they don't yet even conceive of universal moral principles, they follow their 'clan-morality,' etc. – it is hard to see how we can reasonably hold *them* to be committed to the principle that social institutions are legitimate if they would be freely accepted by all agents in an ideal speech situation.

These disagreements about the epistemic status and ultimate grounds of the critical theory need not directly affect the actual practice of Ideologiekritik. Both parties to the disagreement – both the contextualist and the transcendentalist – can agree that Ideologiekritik has a function to perform in situations in which a repressive social practice or institution is considered legitimate by the very agents whose wants and preferences it frustrates because those agents hold some world-picture or set of normative beliefs which they could have acquired only under conditions of coercion. In such a situation, then, a critical theory criticizes a set of beliefs or world-picture as ideological by showing:

(a) that the agents in the society have a set of epistemic principles which contains a provision to the effect that beliefs which are to be sources of legitimation in the society are acceptable *only if* they could have been acquired by the agents under conditions of free and un-coerced discussion;

(b) that the *only* reason the agents accept a particular repressive social institution is that they think this institution is legitimized by a set of beliefs embedded in their world-picture;

(c) that those beliefs could have been acquired by these agents *only* under conditions of coercion.

From this it follows immediately that the beliefs in question are reflectively unacceptable to the agents and that the repressive social institution these beliefs legitimize is not legitimate.

Transcendentalists and contextualists can agree on this model. Con-

[36] TW 78, 72 [T5 103, 98f], LS 38f [T2 22f], TP 31 [T4 25f].
[37] TW 88ff [T5 110ff], KK 79.

textualists will claim that '(a)' is an integral part of *each* critical theory; that '(a)' holds is not something we can automatically presuppose but something which must be established for *each* group to which a critical theory might be addressed. Transcendentalists think that we know apriori that any human group will satisfy '(a)' but they may still agree that it is important to formulate '(a)' separately in each criticial theory, because although *we* may know that any group of agents will have epistemic principles which satisfy '(a)' *they* may not initially know this, and part of the task of the critical theory may be precisely to make them aware of this.

Chapter 1 left open the question of the relation between the three approaches to ideology: the epistemic, the functional, and the genetic approaches. For Habermas, ideology is fundamentally *false* consciousness, the epistemic dimension is the basic one, but the 'falsity' in question is 'reflective unacceptability,' and to say of a form of consciousness that it is reflectively unacceptable is to ascribe to it a 'genetic' property: that it could only have been acquired under conditions of coercion. An ideological form of consciousness 'requires' ignorance of or false belief about its own origin or genesis in the sense that, *given* their epistemic principles, agents would not continue to cling to that form of consciousness, if they knew something about its genesis – namely, if they knew that it could not have arisen in conditions of free discussion.

The functional approach to ideology would then seem to be altogether secondary for Habermas. To be sure, a form of consciousness can't be ideological unless it thwarts some human desires, wants, or preferences. It is also true that *if* a form of consciousness is ideological that means that it will legitimate and stabilize Herrschaft, surplus repression, etc. but what *makes* the form of consciousness an ideology is that it provides *false* legitimation, i.e. that it makes the agents accept as legitimate what if they were perfectly free and completely knowledgeable they would not accept as legitimate. So that an ideological form of consciousness will legitimate Herrschaft seems derivative from the fact that a form of consciousness formed in the ideal speech situation would *not* be one which would legitimate Herrschaft. Still, Habermas obviously thinks that it is not just an accidental or contingent *fact* about human beings that they won't freely and knowingly accept surplus repression, unnecessary inequality, etc.[38] He obviously thinks that it is a mandate of reason itself that rational agents not gratuitously destroy the necessary conditions for the development and exercise of their own rationality, but to accept *surplus* repression or *unnecessary* inequality is to ac-

[38] Vide supra pp. 16–18. I've been assuming that it *is* a fact that agents won't freely agree to unnecessary inequality. But cf. 'Introduction' to Dumont.

cept gratuitous obstacles to the realization of the ideal speech situation. The ideal speech situation, however, is just the ideal condition for the development and exercise of human rationality; we can predict apriori then that *rational* human agents won't *freely* and *knowingly* set up their society so as to prevent themselves from being as rational as possible.

A critical theory was supposed to induce self-reflection and thereby produce enlightenment and emancipation. We may now be in a position to see more clearly how this happens. Self-reflection, the reader will recall,[39]

(a) dissolves pseudo-objectivity and 'objective illusion,'
(b) makes the subject aware of its own origin;
(c) brings to awareness unconscious determinants of consciousness and behavior.

By inducing such self-reflection the critical theory was to bring the agents to realize that the coercion from which they suffer is self-imposed, thereby dissolving the 'power' or 'objectivity' of that coercion and bringing them to a state of greater freedom and knowledge of their true interests.

A critical theory brings to the agents' awareness unconscious determinants of their consciousness and behavior in that it points out to them that their own coercive social institutions are 'determining' them (by distorting the communication structure in the society) to cling to their ideological world-picture. In the initial state the agents falsely think that they are acting freely in accepting the world-picture and acting on it; the critical theory shows them that this is not the case by pointing out social determinants of their consciousness and action of which they were not aware.

In just this way, too, a critical theory makes the subjects in the society aware of their own *origin*.[40] To enlighten the subjects about their own genesis or *origin* is just to explain to them how they became the subjects they are with the beliefs, attitudes, norms, etc. they have. The critical theory shows them under what conditions, in what 'context,' they acquired these beliefs, attitudes, and norms, and how they came to hold their basic world-picture, that is, how they came into being as social subjects.

That still leaves the claim that a critical theory by inducing self-reflection dissolves pseudo-objectivities and 'objective illusion.'[41] What can that mean? To say that *x* is an instance of 'objective illusion' means *both:*

---

[39] Vide supra p. 61.
[40] Cf. TG 230, TP 9f [T4 1f], EI 16, 25ff [T1 8, 15ff].
[41] 'Objektiver Schein' is treated at TG 259, 289, N2 412, EI 81ff [T1 59ff].

(a) x *appears* to be objective, but isn't, i.e. x is a pseudo-objectivity;
(b) *that* x appears to be objective (although it isn't) is itself an objective fact.

If x isn't 'objective' although it appears to be, then presumably it is 'subjective.' Agents who take their own (subjective) activity or the results of that activity to be a 'foreign,' independently existing, natural or 'objective' phenomenon are making an 'objectification mistake'. To take a pseudo-objectivity to be what it appears to be is to make an objectification mistake. Some objectification mistakes might just be random or accidental errors agents make for any of a variety of reasons. But objectification mistakes might also be rooted in the way the society operates, that is, it might not be just an accident that agents in this society tend to make this particular objectification mistake. In particular the society might be so arranged as to insure that almost all the agents make a particular objectification mistake, because it is *necessary* for social reproduction that most of the agents in the society make it. To say in this sense that a particular 'appearance' is 'objective' is to say that it isn't just an accident that things appear that way in the society; *that* things appear that way is a result of the normal operation of the basic social institutions and is perhaps even required for these institutions to operate and reproduce themselves.

That a society is shot through with 'objective illusion' means then that the agents in acting produce a realm of 'objects' which they don't recognize as the result of their own activity, and it is an objective necessity if the society is to reproduce itself that most of the agents in it make this mistake. But what could such a realm of apparent 'objects' (which are really, however, the result of agents' activity) be? One might first think of social practices and institutions. Thus, various Marxists have criticized 'bourgeois' economists and social theorists for making an 'objectification mistake' in taking particular arrangements of capitalist society which result from a particular kind and form of human activity to be invariant, unchangeable natural facts, or results of the operation of 'objective laws of nature.' But note that this is most emphatically not the kind of thing that happens in the cases of ideological delusion we have been considering. The basic assumption of the whole discussion of ideology in this chapter has been that an ideological form of consciousness is one which *legitimizes* a social practice or institution. Now a social arrangement which is mistaken for a natural phenomenon, or a purely 'objective' fact doesn't require or indeed even admit of legitimation. I don't look for legitimizing arguments for hurricanes, floods, or other natural occurrences; I only require legitimation for such things as I *see* to be in my power to change by my action. So it can't be that a critical theory by initiating self-reflection brings the agents in the society to realize that the repressive social institutions from which they suffer are not just objective facts, but are in their power to change. The fact that they demand legitimating arguments for these institutions indicates that they know *that*. So what is it that the agents objectify and about which they make objectification mistakes?

Recall Habermas' general account of 'objectivity.'[42] If an unrestricted community of rational agents investigates a state of affairs under conditions of complete freedom and eventually reaches a stable consensus, the judgment which expresses that consensus is the 'objective truth' about that state of affairs. Natural phenomena, 'facts of nature,' then are 'objective' because there is an 'objective truth' about them, i.e. there is a judgment which expresses the consensus a group of rational agents would form, if it were to investigate the phenomenon under conditions of complete freedom. Consider, then, such a group when it has reached a stable consensus. One can give two apparently contradictory descriptions of the agents in it. Their form of consciousness is 'autonomous,' i.e. the agents formed it in conditions of complete freedom. On the other hand, there is an opinion or judgment on which they are 'destined' to agree. It isn't as if they had a real choice about what opinion they will finally form (provided they wish to remain rational). The only coercion to which they are subject is what Habermas calls 'the peculiar compulsion of the better argument,'[43] but this can be described as a kind of coercion, nonetheless.

An ideological world-picture is 'objective illusion' in the sense that it falsely claims and appears to have exactly the structure described above, that is, it falsely claims that it is the world-picture fully rational agents would find themselves 'compelled' to adopt (by the 'force of the better argument') if they were to engage in unrestricted discussion under ideal conditions.[44] Furthermore this 'appearance' is 'objective' in that it is necessary, if the society is to reproduce itself, that at least most of the members think the basic social institutions are legitimate, and this will be the case only if most of them accept the claim the world-picture makes to 'objective validity' – its 'appearance' – at face-value.[45] The 'self-generated pseudo-objectivities' self-reflection is to 'dissolve' are such 'things' as natural rights, natural law, the 'essence of man,' 'the commodity form,' 'human nature,' etc. that is, they are the 'things'

[42] Vide supra pp. 65f.
[43] WT 240; N2 386.
[44] TW 159f [T1 311f], TP 43 [T4 37f].
[45] TG 246f.

about which the world-picture purports to make objectively valid statements.

By showing the agents in the society that they would not accept their world-picture freely if they were to discuss it under ideal conditions, the critical theory 'dissolves' 'objective illusion,' i.e. it refutes the claim of the world-picture to be objectively valid. If the statements purporting to describe them are shown to have no standing as 'objective knowledge,' i.e. are shown to be statements to which rational agents under ideal conditions would not agree, the pseudo-objects which form part of the content of the ideological form of consciousness are dissolved, too. If all discourse about natural rights is *mere* expression of the preferences of some particular social class, natural rights are 'objects' only of wishful thinking.

Finally, by making the agents realize that the coercion from which they suffer is self-imposed, the critical theory was to break the 'power' or 'objectivity' of that coercion, producing emancipation and enlightenment.

If their situation satisfied the formidable array of conditions which define an 'initial state' of ideological delusion, agents can clearly be enlightened by the 'self reflection' a critical theory sets off. In the initial state their wants and desires were seriously frustrated by a social institution they thought they had an interest in maintaining. Reflection shows them that this is a mistake and that they actually have a real interest in abolishing the social institution in question, which not only frustrates perfectly legitimate wants and preferences, but prevents free communication and discussion.

Even if the agents in the society are enlightened in this way they may be less than fully emancipated. We have been assuming that the *only* reason the agents accept the repressive social institution is that it is legitimized by their ideological world-picture. When they see that that world-picture is false, they realize that the social institution is merely repressive and unacceptable, but this does *not* mean that the repressive social institution will immediately and automatically disappear; powerful social forces may keep the practice or institution in existence despite the fact that increasing numbers of agents realize that it is not legitimate. In fact, repressive social institutions will be kept in existence not merely by a kind of social inertia, but because they foster and promote the real and perceived interests of some particular social group; that group will have every reason to resist the abolition of the institution. The discussion up to now has ignored one important aspect of the situation in which Ideologiekritik becomes necessary: It is the situation of a society split into groups with conflicting interests.

An ideology is not a form of consciousness which merely legitimizes repression, but one which legitimizes *unequal* distribution of normative power. Ideologies arise only in conditions in which unequal distribution of surplus must be legitimized.[46] That the distribution of normative power is 'unequal' means that more is distributed to some group A, than to some other group B. If the social institutions distribute more normative power to A than to B, it will in general be in A's (true or real) interest to retain the normative power its members wield; B will be the group to which the critical theory is 'addressed.' This explains Habermas' claim that an ideology is an apparently autonomous form of consciousness which is however in fact 'bound to some particular interest.'[47] Suppose that a social institution represses members of group B by distributing more normative power to members of A than to members of B. An ideology which legitimizes this institution will have the familiar form: It will claim to be autonomous, but will actually be a form of consciousness the agents could have acquired only under conditions of coercion. The unconscious coercive determinant of their form of consciousness in this case is (ultimately) precisely the social institution which distributes more normative power to members of group A than to members of B. This form of consciousness is thus 'bound to some particular interest' in that it both arises from and legitimizes a situation which is repressive, but in which the repression works to group A's particular advantage.

One way in which Ideologiekritik differs from the other major kind of critical theory, psychoanalysis, is that in cases of neurosis there is often no 'other' agent who benefits from the mystification and repression and who thus has an interest in its continuance.[48] Neurotic repression is self-imposed in a very strong sense; the struggle to overcome it is a struggle with oneself, not with an external – physical or social – reality, and success consists not so much in accomplishing changes in the world as in finding a satisfactory reorganisation of attitudes, habits, feelings, and desires. Self-knowledge leads in a natural way to freedom from self-imposed coercion and freedom from self-imposed coercion *means* reduction in the level of frustration.

This will not necessarily be so in cases of ideological coercion. Ideological coercion is self-imposed – by acting in the way they do, agents constitute it – but the 'objective power' it has over them is not *just* a power which will be automatically dissolved by critical reflection. In act-

---

[46] TW 66 [T5 94f], LS 131f [T2 95f], TG 286, 289.
[47] TW 160 [T1 311f], TP 43 [T4 37].
[48] But cf. Laing and Esterson (1964). For differences between psychoanalysis and social theory vide Giegel in Apel et al. (1971) and TP 34f [T4 28f].

ing in their deluded way the agents have produced a complex of social institutions which cannot now be abolished merely by changes in the agents' beliefs – by the dawning recognition of where their true interests lie. To abolish an established social institution which is deeply rooted in the interests of some social class will in general require more than a change in the form of consciousness of the oppressed; it will require a long course of political action. Until that course of action has been brought to a successful completion, the institution will continue to exist and to exert its baleful influence on even enlightened agents, restricting their freedom and frustrating their desires.

The 'self-imposed coercion' whose power and objectivity reflection can break is the *compulsion to believe* in the legitimacy of the repressive social institutions. Given Habermas' views about the connection between freedom of discussion and legitimacy, it is true that *this* coercion – the coercion to believe – can be effective only for as long as the agents are unaware of its existence or mistake its nature – mistake it for the 'compulsion of the better argument.' By accepting the legitimacy of the repressive social institution the agents have been cooperating in their own frustration. Although reflection alone can't do away with real social oppression, it can free the agents from unconscious *complicity* in thwarting their own legitimate desires. Delegitimization of oppression may be a necessary precondition of the political action which could bring real liberation.

So, in cases of ideological delusion, enlightenment does not automatically bring emancipation in the sense of freedom from the external coercion exercised by social institutions; much less decrease of suffering and frustration. If anything enlightenment is likely to make awareness of frustration rise. Although enlightened agents in a repressive society may know enough to reject their basic social institutions, they may not know much more than that about where their true interests lie, they may not trust themselves to predict what interests they would form in a liberated society. So the process of enlightenment itself may be incomplete until the agents are 'emancipated' not only from complicity in their own oppression, but from the unfree social existence they now lead.

2 CONFIRMATION

If a critical theory is to be cognitive and give us knowledge, it must be the kind of thing that can be true or false, and we would like to know under what conditions it would be falsified and under what conditions confirmed.

A critical theory is a very complicated conceptual object; it is addressed to a particular group of agents in a particular society and aims at being their 'self-consciousness' in a process of successful emancipation and enlightenment. A process of emancipation and enlightenment is a transition from an initial state of bondage, delusion, and frustration to a final state of freedom, knowledge, and satisfaction. A typical critical theory, then, will be composed of three main constituent parts:

(A) A part which shows that a transition from the present state of society (the 'initial state' of the process of emancipation) to some proposed final state is *'objectively'* or 'theoretically' *possible,* i.e. which shows:

    (1) that the proposed final state is inherently possible i.e. that given the present level of development of the forces of production it is possible for society to function and reproduce itself in this proposed state;

    (2) that it is possible to transform the present state into the proposed final state (by means of specified institutional or other changes).

(B) A part which shows that the transition from the present state to the proposed final state is *'practically necessary,'* i.e. that

    (1) the present state is one of reflectively unacceptable frustration, bondage, and illusion, i.e. (a) the present social arrangements cause pain, suffering, and frustration; (b) the agents in the society only accept the present arrangements and the suffering they entail because they hold a particular world-picture; (c) that world-picture is not reflectively acceptable to the agents, i.e. it is one they acquired only because they were in conditions of coercion;

    (2) the proposed final state will be one which will lack the illusions and unnecessary coercion and frustration of the present state; the proposed final state will be one in which it will be easier for the agents to realize their true interests.

(C) A part which asserts that the transition from the present state to the proposed final state can come about only if the agents adopt the critical theory as their 'self-consciousness' and act on it.

If one thinks of this abstract scheme as filled in with a particular content, with Marxism, for instance, then the 'initial state' is the present capitalist mode of production and the proposed 'final state' is the classless society.

Without part (A), the critical theory of society would be no more than another utopian fantasy, a dream of an ideal state of which we could say neither whether it was possible nor how it might be realized. Part

(A) is the part of the critical theory most like 'empirical social science.'[49] There are no special epistemological problems involved in determining what would count as confirmation of the claim that a classless society could reproduce itself and what would count as disconfirmation.

Although it is important to avoid utopianism, it is at least equally important to avoid scientism – the view that all knowledge of society is scientific knowledge. The members of the Frankfurt School take it as an important distinguishing feature of their 'critical' version of Marxism (and a sign of its superiority over more orthodox versions) that they do not categorically predict the 'inevitable' coming of the classless society. Marxism as a theory of society claims to give *knowledge* of the *necessity* of a transformation of the present social order into a classless society. The members of the Frankfurt School wish to gloss the 'necessity' in question as what they call 'practical necessity.'[50] That is, the Marxist knows that the agents in the society have an overwhelming real interest in bringing about a classless society. The orthodox Marxist, however, is committed to scientism, and so does not admit the possibility of *knowledge* of 'practical necessity.' So if the coming of the classless society is 'necessary' that must mean that it can be predicted theoretically as 'inevitable.' From the fact, however, that the agents have an overwhelming practical interest in bringing about an objectively possible transformation, it does not follow that the transformation is inevitable. Whether or not it will occur depends on all kinds of other facts which the theory may not allow us to predict; in particular it depends on whether large numbers of agents find the critical theory plausible, adopt it, and act on it effectively. Sometimes the members of the Frankfurt School seem almost to be suggesting that one couldn't possibly predict the free decisions of large numbers of agents. It is perhaps more charitable to take them as asserting that no matter how strong our grounds for predicting that the agents will adopt the critical theory, that decision is not 'inevitable,' or as emphasizing that the real *point* of the *critical* theory is not to make categorical predictions, but to enlighten agents about how they ought rationally to act to realize their own best interests.

Parts (B) and (C), then, are the distinctive features of the critical theory. Obviously it is a necessary condition of acceptability that part (B) of a critical theory contain no simple factual errors. If the critical theory asserts that the agents in the society are communicating 'under coercion' because 85% of the newspapers, magazines, and radio stations in the country are owned by one large company which uses them to dis-

---

[49] The 'critical' version of Marxism is supposed to be an 'empirisch überprüfbare Geschichtsphilosophie' TP 428, 434, WL 53 [T6 51f].
[50] TP 412f, WL 57ff [T6 55ff].

seminate views conducive to the interests of some particular social group, it must be the case that one company owns 85% of the newspapers, magazines, and radio stations in the country.

Yet part (B) of the critical theory is not easy to assimilate to the empiricist model. 'This world-picture is reflectively unacceptable to these agents' implies, as we know, 'These agents would not have acquired this world-picture in conditions of freedom.' The critical theory depends crucially on a theory of freedom and coercion.[51] Where does such a theory come from and what is its status?

The critical theory claims to derive its views on freedom and coercion from the agents to whom it is addressed, that is, it claims that its embedded theory of freedom and coercion is merely a clearer formulation of views implicit in the action and form of consciousness of the agents to whom it is addressed. This is yet another instance of the principle of 'internal criticism': The agents themselves must be the final judges of whether or not they are being coerced and whether or not they are free.

To say that the agents themselves must be the *final* judges of their own freedom or coercion is, however, most decidedly *not* to say that their own immediate judgments about conditions of freedom or coercion are definitive. If that were the case, Ideologiekritik would be superfluous. The point of a theory of ideology is that agents are sometimes suffering from a coercion of which they are not immediately aware. The agents are the final judges of their own freedom or coercion only in that there is no appeal from their perfectly free, fully informed, and thoroughly considered judgment.

A critical theory, then, is not acceptable unless it is empirically adequate and unless it enjoys the free assent of the agents to whom it is addressed,[52] i.e. unless the agents to whom it is addressed agree (after thorough consideration in conditions of perfect information and full freedom) to the views about freedom and coercion expressed in it. What are the 'conditions of perfect information and full freedom' in which agents' expressed assent or dissent is real, i.e. free assent or dissent? The critical theory itself, of course, contains full and clear specifications of what count as conditions of perfect information and complete freedom,[53] but to use these specifications at *this* point would seem to involve a circularity. If I don't from the start agree that conditions C are conditions of freedom, I may be unimpressed by the fact (if it is a fact) that if I *were* to be in conditions C, I would *then* agree that they are

[51] WL 5of [T6 48f].
[52] TP 36, 41ff [T4 31, 36ff], WL 41f [T6 40f].
[53] Vide supra, pp. 63ff.

conditions of freedom. If an Ik 'critical theorist' asserted that if I were to live my whole life in conditions like those in which the Ik live I would realize that those are conditions of freedom, I might well agree, but this would in no way suggest to me that the views about freedom I would form in those conditions are the 'right' ones.

At the beginning of this chapter I reported the Frankfurt claim that critical theories differ from 'scientific' theories in basic cognitive structure and in mode of confirmation.[54] Scientific theories are cognitively acceptable if they are empirically accurate and are confirmed by observation and experiment; critical theories are acceptable if they are empirically accurate and if their 'objects,' the agents to whom they are addressed, would freely agree to them. A critical theory addressed to the proletariat is confirmed, if its description of the objective situation of the proletariat in society is confirmed by normal observational means, and if the members of the proletariat freely assent to the theory, in particular to the views about freedom and coercion expressed in the theory. For most 'scientific' theories the question of whether or not the 'objects of research' would freely assent to the theory doesn't even arise; planets, genes, microscopic particles, etc. can't assent or dissent.

A critical theory is structurally different from a scientific theory in that it is 'reflective' and not 'objectifying,' that is, it is not just a theory about some objects different from itself, it is also a theory about social theories, how they arise, how they can be applied, and the conditions under which they are acceptable. The central part of a critical theory is the criterion of acceptability for beliefs it presents. To be sure, the critical theory *presents* this criterion as one it found the agents to whom the theory is addressed already using, but the critical theory does *not* merely describe this criterion non-committally, it uses it *as true* (or at least as the best approximation available). The critical theory doesn't just assert that the poor benighted creatures to whom it is addressed would, given their bizarre epistemic principles, find this particular ideological world-picture unacceptable; it also asserts that it *is* unacceptable. The agents would find it unacceptable and they would be right. The critical theory must, therefore, itself be acceptable by the criterion it extracts from the agents' behavior and form of consciousness, and uses to undermine their ideological world-picture. The critical theory does not, then, like objectifying theories, purport merely to give information about society, its members, and their form of consciousness, it also purports to provide the criterion by which to evaluate whether or not the critical theory itself, and the information it provides are acceptable. There would

[54] Vide supra, pp. 55f.

seem, then, to be no neutral way to evaluate the critical theory. If one uses the criterion of acceptability it provides, it won't be at all surprising that the critical theory qualifies as 'acceptable,' but to use any *other* criterion seems to build rejection of the critical theory into the test conditions. Certainly a critical theory must *at least* satisfy its own standard of acceptability, i.e. it must be true that, if the agents to whom the theory is addressed were to consider the matter in circumstances the theory defines as 'conditions of perfect freedom,' they would assent to the views about freedom and coercion embodied in the theory.

The criterion of free assent applies not only to the central epistemological apparatus of the critical theory, but to other parts of it as well. Up to now we have been making an assumption which has simplified the argument, but which must now be investigated more closely.

It has been assumed that the agents to whom the critical theory will be addressed *both* know that they are suffering pain and frustration *and* know the source of that frustration. They know which social institution is repressing them, but accept that repression and that institution because of the world-picture they have adopted. The critical theory 'has its origin in the experience of pain and repression.'[55] The experience of pain and frustration is what gives the agents addressed motivation to consider the critical theory and to act on it to change their social arrangements. I will call the situation in which the agents both know that they are frustrated and know the institutional cause of their frustration the 'standard' situation.

Of course, it is possible to *experience* suffering and frustration *without* knowing the ultimate cause of one's frustration, especially if the cause is some large-scale social institution like 'private property,' or 'the state.' Agents in this situation may still be ideologically deluded – indeed one might wish to claim that they are even more deeply deluded than the agents in the 'standard' situation because they cannot even correctly locate the source of their frustration – and may have in their experienced pain a strong motivation to adopt and act on the critical theory. In this case the critical theory will have to include explicitly in part (B) an argument designed to show the agents what particular social institution or arrangement is the source of their suffering. Similarly, if the agents have a false theory (rather than no beliefs at all) about the cause of their suffering, e.g. if they think it is a punishment from God, or part of the unavoidable suffering which is the lot of all humans, the critical theory must first disabuse them of this false theory before proceeding to 'emancipate' them. Neither in the case in which the

[55] EI 344, 349 [T1 283f, 287f], WL 47ff [T6 45ff].

agents have no beliefs nor in the case in which they have false beliefs is a real extension of the critical theory necessary. The critical theory is committed to the existence of an appropriate causal relation between some social institution and the agents' suffering in *any* case, and the only question is whether or not it is worth while including a statement of this relation in the critical theory as presented to the agents to be emancipated; if they already know that this relation holds, they don't need to be told that it does, but even in the 'standard case' the critical theory is falsified if it turns out that it designated, either explicitly or implicitly, the wrong social institution as the source of the agents' suffering.

Finally some members of the Frankfurt School countenance even 'deeper' kinds of ideological delusion than the ones already treated. Marcuse and Adorno, in particular, think that modern industrial societies can exercise such extensive control over even the inner life of their members as to prevent them from becoming fully aware of the fact that they are frustrated and miserable. Agents in such societies are deprived even of a full and immediate experience of their unhappiness. Suppose that the society is so powerful that it can prevent agents from recognizing and expressing some wishes and desires they have. It is likely, then, that frustration of these desires will not be something which is ever allowed to come to full consciousness: clear recognition of the frustration might lead to recognition of the inadmissible unconscious desire. The result will be vague malaise, free-floating dissatisfaction, irrational behavior patterns, etc. – in short, a situation of frustration and unhappiness which is not recognized for what it is.

In this situation the first task of a critical theory would be to make the agents aware that some of their (unconscious) desires were being frustrated. Proponents of the critical theory attribute these unconscious desires to the agents on the basis of the agents' overt behavior; the most obvious way to try to convince the members of the society that some of their unconscious desires are being frustrated is to present them with this evidence drawn from their own behavior. Since the principle of 'free assent' applies to this part of the critical theory, too, the agents to whom the critical theory is addressed must freely recognize the 'unconscious desires' attributed to them as their own, and must freely agree that they are unhappy and frustrated. Only when the agents have agreed that they are unhappy can the critical theory proceed to reveal the source of their suffering in social institutions which falsely lay claim to legitimacy.

Suppose, however, that the agents in the society really *are* fully satisfied with their lives and show no behavioral signs of hidden frustration.

Perhaps their social institutions are so powerful and effective they can completely prevent the members of the society from forming, even unconsciously, desires which cannot be satisfied within the present institutional framework. Is this an appropriate 'initial state' of bondage and delusion from which the agents must be emancipated? Often the situations of 'ideological delusion' Marcuse describes seem to be not so much ones in which the agents have unconscious, unfulfilled desires – in which they are unhappy or frustrated – as ones in which they lead shallow or uninteresting lives, or have a low level of aspirations. If the agents sincerely report themselves to be satisfied with their lives, and if we have no behavioral evidence for hidden frustration, by what standard can we adjudge these lives 'poor' or 'shallow,' and the agents in need of 'enlightenment?' The answer is that we can extract from 'the cultural tradition' standards of what the 'good life' is.[56] These views can be found expressed in certain works of art, and in religious and metaphysical doctrines, or can be derived from particular aesthetic or religious experiences. To a large extent these images of the good life are utopian; they describe states of affairs which could not exist. There is no New Jerusalem, but agents can be quite happy although they don't live there. In fact, they may quite reasonably prefer *not* to live in the New Jerusalem of their tradition; certainly the fact that they are not pining away after it does not, if their lives are otherwise satisfactory, seem serious grounds for criticizing them or thinking them in need of enlightenment. In some societies there may be a presumption that as much of the utopian content of its tradition as *can* be realized *is* realized. If this presumption exists, the critical theory might enlighten the agents about how much more of the utopian content of their tradition they could realize than they do.

This approach to Ideologiekritik from the utopian content of the cultural tradition may seem to be a rather elitist enterprise. Society is criticized not because of the experienced suffering it imposes on some oppressed group but because it appears to fail to satisfy the neurasthenic sensibilities of a cultural elite. To be sure, 'Things are horrible and we have been prevented from realizing that they needn't be quite so horrible' probably yields stronger motives for action than 'Things are fine, and we have been prevented from realizing how much better they could be,' but there is no inherent reason for this approach to be elitist. The agents in the society may be perfectly content, but, if they were released from some unperceived coercion, they might come to realize that their

[56]TW 78, 89 [T5 103f, 111f], TG 267, EI 340, 344, 350 [T1 280, 283f, 288], TP 42, 267f [T4 36f, 239], KK 331ff, WL 74f [T6 72f].

mode of existence is lacking in dignity, or self-directedness, does not provide satisfactory aesthetic experiences, etc.; *any* agent might be quite capable of realizing this and of developing the appropriate new desires.

So we have considered four quite different 'initial states':

(1) agents are suffering and know what social institution or arrangement is the cause;

(2) agents know that they are suffering, but either don't know what the cause is or have a false theory about the cause;

(3) agents are apparently content, but analysis of their behavior shows them to be suffering from hidden frustration of which they are not aware;

(4) agents are actually content, but only because they have been prevented from developing certain desires which in the 'normal' course of things they would have developed, and which cannot be satisfied within the framework of the present social order.

Habermas has two slightly different descriptions of the effect of a critical theory: (A) the critical theory aims at reduction of identifiable suffering, (B) the critical theory initiates a 'Prozeß der Selbstaufklärung vergesellschafteter Individuen über das was sie wollen würden, wenn sie wüßten, was sie wollen könnten.'[57] (A) fits (1) and (2) and can be stretched to encompass (3) but not (4). (B), on the other hand, fits case (4) quite well, but not case (1). In case (1) the agents' problem is not that they don't know what they *could* want – they know that what they want is an abatement of suffering; what they don't know is rather that they could act so as to alleviate their suffering in a way which is legitimate, rational, and compatible with the pursuit of their real interests.

Still (B) expresses, albeit in an obscure and inadequate way, the important fact that what is basic in *all* cases of ideological delusion is that the agents' form of consciousness is artificially limited, i.e. that they suffer from restrictions on what they can perceive as real possibilities for themselves.[58] Agents in case (4) have a restricted perception of their possibilities in that they cannot even conceive of having certain desires which under normal conditions they would have developed. Agents in case (1) have 'restricted possibilities' because they falsely see themselves as having no legitimate alternative to accepting their suffering.

Case (4) is the nightmare which haunts the Frankfurt School. It is the

---

[57] That is, a critical theory initiates a 'process of self-enlightenment of socialized individuals about what they would want if they knew what they could want.' TG 281, TW 118f, 134ff, 137 [T5 160f, 72ff, 74], TG 146f.

[58] At EI 281 [T1 229] Habermas speaks of the 'dogmatische Beschränkung eines falschen Bewußtseins.' Vide N2 380, 412, TG 279, 258f.

specter of a society where social control is so total and so effective that members can be prevented from even forming desires which cannot be easily satisfied, a society of happy slaves, genuinely content with their chains. This is a nightmare, not a realistic view of a state of society which is at present possible. Although the total control envisaged in case (4) is probably not possible, we may wish to criticize some societies *both* for frustrating some desires and for preventing others from even being formed.

To the extent to which the initial state approximates case (3) or case (4) the first task of the critical theory will be to increase the agents awareness of their own pain, frustration or unhappiness or to make them dissatisfied with the limitations of their present mode of existence. It should be no surprise, then, if proponents of a critical theory encounter 'resistance' among those to whom the theory is addressed; the more so, as in many cases the agents will not only be suffering from ideological delusion, but will also be under the influence of various kinds of social 'opiates,' that is, they will be bound to the present society, not only by belief in its legitimacy, but also by a series of 'false' modes of gratification which would be jeopardized by emancipation.[59]

The analysis of the 'ideological form of consciousness' of any actual society will, then, be quite a complicated matter, involving an account of conscious and unconscious frustration accepted because of normative beliefs, claims about the kinds of desires the agents in the society would develop (but have been prevented from developing), and descriptions of the operations of 'false' modes of gratification. Use of opiates is an embellishment on the basic pattern of ideological delusion: legitimation of repression and suffering through restriction of consciousness. Nevertheless the principle of 'free assent' still applies; a mode of gratification is an 'opiate' only if the agents themselves would agree under the appropriate conditions of full information and complete freedom that it is not in their interest to indulge in it.

Part (C) of the critical theory is adapted from Lukács. In *Geschichte und Klassenbewußtsein* Lukács claims that the capitalist mode of production can be abolished only as the intended result of action by a proletariat with the correct class-consciousness.[60] The 'critical theory' is to supply that correct class-consciousness.

Lukács himself admits that earlier revolutionary transformations of society were brought about by agents who had no correct understanding of their own interests or class-situation. The transformation of feu-

---

[59] 'Ersatzbefriedigung' is discussed at ZL 181f, TG 258f, KK 79.
[60] Esp. the chapters 'Klassenbewußtsein' and 'Funktionswechsel des historischen Materialismus.' Vide supra p. 24.

dalism into capitalism took place as a result of action by members of the bourgeoisie who did not know what they were doing, who were acting out fantasies, and yet succeeded in creating a new society suited to the realization of their class interests. Why might something similar not be possible for the proletariat under capitalism? Of course an enlightened form of consciousness may be supremely useful in orienting the action of the proletariat and the proletariat may be extremely unlikely to succeed in abolishing the capitalist mode of production without a correct view of their own interests, but that is not at issue. The question is whether, and if so in what sense, the adoption of the critical theory is strictly *necessary* for real emancipation.[61]

Even if it isn't strictly necessary that the agents accept and act on the critical theory – even if emancipation could have come about in some other way – it still may be a condition of acceptability of a critical theory that it be the kind of thing agents *could* adopt as their self-consciousness. That is, a critical theory must be expressed in a form comprehensible to the agents addressed, and which allows them to recognize it as a description of their own situation and use it as a guide for action. It isn't clear to me why the members of the Frankfurt School make such heavy weather of this 'hermeneutic' requirement.[62] Obviously any theory which enjoys the 'free assent' of the agents to whom it is addressed will afortiori satisfy this 'hermeneutic' requirement.

A critical theory must be empirically confirmed in the normal way; it also asserts of itself that it can be *definitively* confirmed or disconfirmed only by being freely accepted or rejected by agents in the ideal speech situation. We are not and are unlikely ever to be in the ideal speech situation but still we may be able to tell in a rough way which concrete situations are closer and which less close approximations of the ideal speech situation; the closer a given situation approximates the ideal speech situation, the greater weight the agents' expressed assent or dissent should have.

Suppose, then, that the agents adopt the critical theory and act to put its recommended course of action into effect (following part (A) (2) of the critical theory). Then the proposed 'final state' must eventuate; if it does not, or if the final state turns out to be inherently unstable, the critical theory is disconfirmed. If the proposed final state is reached (and is stable), the agents in this state must freely agree that they have been enlightened and emancipated, and that the critical theory gives a correct account of the process of emancipation and enlightenment.

[61] TP 33 [T4 27f].
[62] But vide infra pp. 92ff.

That is, they must agree that their former state was one of bondage, frustration, and delusion, as described by the critical theory and that their present state is one of increased freedom and satisfaction, and one in which they have a more correct view of their true interests. Finally they must freely acknowledge that knowledge of the critical theory and the process of reflection it initiated was the mechanism of their emancipation. If the agents refuse any part of this complex free assent – if, for instance, having experienced the 'final state' they decide that they were better off back in the original state – the critical theory is disconfirmed.

The emancipation at issue here must be 'real' emancipation. That is, it is not enough that the oppressed agents no longer voluntarily cooperate in their own frustration, there must be a change in the basic social institutions which does away with the experienced suffering and the restriction of human possibilities which motivated the agents to adopt the critical theory.[63]

The initial state of ideological delusion was one of *differential* oppression, that is, one in which some groups benefited more than – or even at the direct expense of – others. The critical theory is addressed to the members of the disadvantaged and oppressed group, but that means that the 'emancipation' to which the critical theory is to lead will deprive dominant groups of some perceived advantages. Emancipatory transformation of society need not be violent – the privileged *may* freely acknowledge the correctness of the critical theory and voluntarily relinquish their privileges – but it would not be at all surprising if it usually was. Must the agents who belong to the advantaged group also freely assent to the critical theory and agree that the process it initiates is one of emancipation and enlightenment?

There seems to be a slight ambiguity in the treatment of the requirement of 'free assent.' Habermas' general view is that a theory is 'cognitively acceptable' if it would enjoy the universal assent of *all* agents in the ideal speech situation. On the other hand, in the discussion of confirmation it is easy to slip into speaking of a critical theory as acceptable if the agents to whom it is addressed freely assent to it, regardless of what the other members of the society think – after all, *they* are the agents whose suffering the critical theory purports to alleviate and whose interests it claims to foster. Since the critical theory is not ad-

---

[63] Habermas states several times, to be sure, that the 'practical results' of self-reflection are 'Einstellungsänderungen' (TP 44 [T4 39f], PS 236, 238, 248, 250f, 253, 255 [T3 199, 201, 210ff, 215f]), and although changes in the agents beliefs and attitudes *may* be sufficient in the psychoanalytic case, they cannot be the final goal of a critical social theory: If the coercive institutions of the society are intact, it is not enough for the oppressed agents to have gained an inner freedom from compulsion to believe in their legitimacy. Vide KK 392f, TP 9f [T4 1f].

dressed to them, it isn't even entirely clear what form the assent of the dominant class to the critical theory might take: Must the dominant class agree that *they too* have been emancipated and enlightened, or is it sufficient for them to agree that the oppressed have been emancipated and enlightened? If the critical theory is correct, the members of the dominant class are suffering from a constricted form of consciousness – they live in a society in which the communication structure is distorted for everyone – but this restriction does not frustrate their desires, rather it operates to their benefit.

It is the clear intention of the critical theory that if the agents in a particular society have been emancipated from ideological delusion and coercion, they must *all,* including the former dominant class, agree that they prefer their present emancipated state to the former 'initial' state, and that they have come to a more correct view of where their true interests lie. How is this possible?

To say that the ideological delusion works 'to the benefit and advantage' of the members of the dominant group means only that *in the given social system as then constituted* it is better to be a member of the dominant than of the oppressed group, i.e. that in *this* social order it is well to have as much normative power as possible. This in no way implies that the members of the dominant group are not themselves also massively frustrated, and also implies nothing about what social system they *would* prefer, if they had free choice. *If* the only choice is to be a helot or to be one of the Homoioi, one can understand that agents join the Homoioi, although – if it were possible – they might prefer to live in Athens, even as metics. So if the process a critical theory initiates is truly one of emancipation and enlightenment, the members of the dominant class should at the end of the process recognize and agree that their privileges were opiates, modes of gratification which served to mask the much more serious and pervasive forms of frustration from which they suffered.

If the critical theory does become the 'self-consciousness' of a successful process of emancipation and enlightenment, that means that it becomes the ideology in a *positive* sense of the group to which it is addressed.[64] An ideology in the pejorative sense is not *just* false consciousness; it is 'reason,' albeit in a 'distorted' or 'irrational' form. Agents whose form of consciousness is ideological aren't *completely* deluded about their wants, needs and interests; if they were, they would be beyond the reach of the 'internal criticism' which is the main method of Ideologiekritik. Ideologiekritik is possible only if we can extract the very instruments of criticism from the agents' own form of conscious-

[64] Vide supra pp. 22–6.

ness – from their views about the good life, from the notions of freedom, truth, and rationality embedded in their normative epistemology. It is the particular insidiousness of ideology that it turns human desires and aspirations against themselves and uses them to fuel repression. These aspirations and desires do find a kind of expression in the ideology, and, to the extent they do, the ideology is said to have a 'utopian kernel' which it is the task of the critical theory to set free.[65] In describing the genesis of an ideological form of consciousness the critical theory shows how it was subjectively rational for the agents to acquire it – in what way it seemed to allow the development, expression, and satisfaction of their basic desires within the framework of their normative beliefs – but the critical theory must also show in what way the particular form of expression these needs and desires found is self-destructive, how it prevented the development of some desires, and frustrated the satisfaction of others. The positive task of the critical theory is to 'save the utopian content' of the cultural tradition, i.e. to 'separate' the underlying genuine human wants, values, needs, and aspirations from their ideological mode of expression;[66] only then can agents hope to attain correct perception of their wants and needs, and form correct views about their real interests.

3 EPISTEMOLOGY

Having seen what a critical theory is and how it is confirmed, two questions remain:

(A) Is a critical theory a kind of knowledge, cognition, or Wissenschaft?
(B) Is a critical theory different from scientific theories in its basic epistemic structure?

For Habermas a 'Wissenschaft' is a body of systematically interconnected propositions which gives reliable guidance for successful action, and which satisfies certain conditions of 'publicity' and intersubjectivity. That is, a proposed Wissenschaft must be connected with a realm of potential action, and we must have relatively clear, 'public' criteria for success in acting in this realm. The bridge either holds up when the truck drives over it, or it collapses; someone who strikes some keys on the piano has either succeeded in producing a major triad in root position, or has not; the bomb either explodes when it hits the hospital, or it does not. We have relatively clear, agreed-on criteria for when agents

[65] TP 42, 267f [T4 37, 239f], EI 340, 344 [T1 280, 283f], PP 29ff, WL 51ff, 63, 104f [T6 50ff, 60f, 99f].
[66] ZL 177, 181f, ZR 50, WL 74f, [T6 72].

have produced a stable bridge, a major triad in root position, or a bombed hospital. Furthermore, if a body of propositions is to constitute a Wissenschaft, it must not be just a black-box which appears on the scene from nowhere and inexplicably turns out to be a reliable guide for successful action; Wissenschaft is not revelation. A Wissenschaft must have an argumentative structure which allows those who have mastered it to give some account of how and why it 'works,' of the relation of its parts to each other, to show the evidence for particular assertions and defend them from criticism, etc. and this must take place relative to some intersubjectively recognized standards of argumentative cogency and evidence.

Traditional empiricism mistook this requirement of 'publicity' and connected it not with the possibility of universal free intersubjective agreement, but with 'observation,' and so ultimately with a kind of direct sensory stimulation. This mistake is easy to make. Observation statements are probably the most striking case of statements on which there will be widespread intersubjective agreement, but the reason they play such a central role in our empirical knowledge is not that they 'stand closest to sensation,' but that consensus about them is most widespread and unproblematic.[67]

Critical theories are connected with the realm of 'emancipatory action.' Are there clear, 'public' criteria for success and failure of emancipation? If to have public criteria for success or failure just means that all agents can agree on whether or not they have been emancipated, then there would seem to be nothing in *principle* to prevent a critical theory from satisfying the condition of publicity. Emancipation can miscarry: the agents may steadfastly refuse to accept the views about freedom embodied in the critical theory, or they may recognize that they acquired certain beliefs or traits under conditions of coercion, but maintain that they would have acquired them anyway, even if they had been in circumstances of complete freedom; finally, when they have experienced the state of 'freedom' the critical theory proposes, they may discover that it imposes unexpected and intolerable burdens on them and must be abandoned. Whether the process of emancipation is a failure or a success is something on which agents may be able to agree.

Still one might think that this misses the point of the requirement of publicity. Even if it isn't directly tied to sensation, it can't just mean that the agents would reach consensus. That criteria are 'public' must mean that they have some kind of independence of the particular theory being evaluated, that they can be formulated in a way which makes

---

[67] Quine's 'Epistemology Naturalized' in Quine (1969), esp. pp. 84ff.

them neutral between competing views.[68] We know what it would be like for the bridge to remain standing no matter what, if any, views we might have about how to go about constructing it. The criteria for success of emancipation don't usually have this kind of neutrality or independence. To the extent to which the critical theory is directed toward the alleviation of experienced suffering, that experience will give us a clear negative criterion of success of emancipation, but in most cases, as we have seen, the critical theory is directed at a restriction of consciousness which causes frustration of which the agents are not fully aware. In that case the very standards of 'success' of emancipation emerge only in the course of adopting and acting on the critical theory.[69]

The neutrality of 'public standards' ought also to be a cultural neutrality or independence of a particular cultural context. Determination of whether action has or has not been successful ought to depend as little as possible on the acquisition and development of the specific habits, attitudes, and skills of a particular culture; it should require only a very 'restricted' kind of experience immediately available to all human agents regardless of the particular cultural content of their form of consciousness.

To determine whether or not emancipatory action has been successful will require just the subtle, sympathetic assimilation of complicated, inexplicit cultural patterns and attitudes that appeal to 'restricted scientific experience' was to exclude. The central and characteristic statements of a critical theory do seem more helplessly embedded in a particular historical and cultural context than scientific theories are. In the case of simple judgments of direct observation 'real' assent seems to coincide with expressed assent in a wide and varied range of circumstances. Even in very repressive societies it seems possible to get 'real' assent to simple empirical propositions; we know that this assent is given in extremely coercive social circumstances – the agents may know it, too – but that doesn't matter. This contrasts strongly with the situation for critical theories; assent to or dissent from them is extremely sensitive to any kind of coercion in the social 'environment,' and that

[68] Vide supra pp. 79f.
[69] There is one rather striking passage in EI which seems to be incompatible with the view I am presenting here. At EI 325 [T1 266] in speaking of psychoanalytic 'interpretations' Habermas says that in the case of such interpretations 'Erfolg und Mißerfolg sind hier nicht . . . intersubjektiv verifizierbar.' A parallel passage at ZL 302 states that in psychoanalytic cases: 'die Kriterien des Erfolgs lassen sich nicht operationalisieren; Erfolge und Mißerfolge sind nicht, wie etwa die Beseitigung von Symptomen, intersubjektiv feststellbar.' So I take it that in denying that 'interpretations' are 'intersubjektiv verifizierbar' Habermas is merely asserting that we can't give *operational*, public criteria of success. The whole point is that there can be other kinds of public criteria of success of action. Vide PS 238 [T3 201].

expressed assent or dissent is 'real' assent or dissent is not lightly to be taken for granted – circumstances in which the agents will be capable of 'real' assent or dissent must be carefully and delicately constructed.

Even if these differences between scientific and critical theories are granted, they seem to be rather differences of degree than categorical differences between 'knowledge' and something else. If knowledge is basically whatever gives 'successful orientation in action' on which there can be free intersubjective agreement – if the existence of pre-given, 'neutral' standards of success is a side-issue, important only insofar as these standards might contribute to the 'freedom' of intersubjective agreement – then a critical theory would seem to be a form of knowledge. The requirement of 'reflective acceptability' is a *cognitive* requirement if the agents can freely agree on what parts of their form of consciousness are reflectively unacceptable, and if this agreement can be used as a guide to action which they can all agree is successful, e.g. if they can agree that giving up the reflectively unacceptable part of their form of consciousness eventually results in a reduced level of frustration.

Critical and scientific theories are alike in a trivial and uninteresting sense in that both are forms of 'empirical' knowledge – both are based on and can be confirmed only by experience. However, the 'experience' on which a critical theory is based includes not only observation but also the 'Erfahrung der Reflexion.'[70] Whatever differences in epistemic status or cognitive structure exist between scientific and critical theories are to be attributed to the role 'reflection' plays in the confirmation of critical theories.

Critical theories purport to show that such parts of a form of consciousness as attitudes or normative beliefs are 'false,' and so the real problem would seem to be that of showing that a critical theory can be a kind of knowledge or cognition at all. If a critical theory is a kind of knowledge (and if we reject naturalism), it seems obvious that it won't be a kind of *scientific* knowledge: How would one go about examining 'instances' of normative beliefs? How would one apply the hypothetico-deductive method? Ideological beliefs and attitudes aren't refuted by pointing out observed negative instances, but by inducing reflection, i.e. by making the agents who hold these beliefs and attitudes aware of how they could have acquired them.

The crux of the purported difference between critical and scientific theories, then, is the claim that knowledge of how agents could have acquired certain beliefs, e.g. normative beliefs, is not a kind of knowl-

[70] El 9 [T1 vii], cf. PS 161ff, 238 [T3 136ff, 201].

edge based on observation. What is it about 'observation' which makes
it an inadequate or inappropriate mode of access to agents' acquisition
of beliefs? The members of the Frankfurt School assume that we can
speak of 'observation' only when the object or state of affairs observed
is independent of the act of observing, i.e. when the object or state of
affairs observed is not essentially changed and is certainly not created
or brought into being by the act of observing; this is what makes observation an appropriate foundation for 'objectifying' science.[71]

How, then, do agents acquire normative beliefs and attitudes?
Through various more or less complicated processes of socialization,
through conversations with other agents about their experiences, and
through the internalization of such conversations which is individual
thought. So to know how agents could have acquired beliefs one would
have to be able to know the outcomes of possible conversations or discussions conducted under various conditions. This means that one
knows how various external factors in the agents' situation will affect
the outcome, but it also means that one knows something about their
epistemic principles and their perception of their own situation, about
what they take to be plausible motives for action, cogent arguments,
good reasons for belief, relevant considerations, etc. One can't, of
course, observe the agents' normative epistemology or their beliefs
about what are plausible motives for action, at best one can observe
their behavior, including their verbal behavior. It seems unlikely, however, that observation of behavior alone (even including observation of
verbal behavior) could provide grounds for exact knowledge of what
sorts of arguments the agents will find cogent or persuasive. The dismal
failure of behaviorism to give a convincing account of such phenomena
is not encouraging. If one wishes to find out how the agents view the
world and what they are likely to find convincing in discussion, one
must enter into their mode of life by interacting with them – discussing
the weather with them, playing with their children, planning joint en-
terprises with them, consuming the local narcotic drug with them, etc.
This kind of long-term interaction is not, it is claimed, just a course of
observation and experiment, and the reason for this is the particularly
intimate active involvement of the 'observer' in what is 'observed.'[72] At
any point in the course of this 'interaction,' I, the participant 'observer,'
may attribute to the other agents a normative epistemology, a way of
perceiving their own situation, and a set of beliefs about what are good
reasons, cogent arguments, comprehensible motives, etc. My grounds
for this attribution will be that acting on it results in smooth, fluent, and

[71] N2 394f.
[72] ZL 138ff, 188ff, 219.

'undisturbed' interaction. But, as we know,[73] with sufficient ingenuity I could come up with another set of beliefs about reasons, motives, perceptions, etc. incompatible with the first set and yet compatible with all the observational evidence. Attribution of beliefs of this sort is observationally underdetermined. I attribute to the others *that* set of views (a) which is compatible with all the observational evidence about their behavior, and (b) which makes them most comprehensible *to me*, i.e. which makes them least bizarre and most 'normal' by *my* standards of what are reasonable, comprehensible views about motives, arguments, reasons, and evidence. If I change my views on these matters – if, for instance, I decide that motives I once thought bizarre and perverse are in fact natural and reasonable – I may immediately change the beliefs about human motives I attribute to the 'others' although their behavior has not discernibly changed at all. I need not, of course, think that they share all of my particular views, but the views *I* am willing to act on impose *some* limits on what I can find plausible to attribute to them. If I change my views about what are good reasons for acting, what is a possible way of looking at the world, what are comprehensible human motives, etc. this may be as a direct result of encounter with other agents with whom I am trying to interact and whose behavior I must therefore interpret. The experience of agents avowing and apparently acting on what seemed to me antecedently to be bizarre and incomprehensible motives may eventually change my views about human motivation. This yields yet another sense of 'reflection:' The motives, epistemic principles, etc. I attribute to others reflect my own in that I have no alternative but to impose my views on them in interpreting their action, but my motives, views about motives, epistemic principles, etc. reflect 'the others' in that they are the result of successive attempts to interpret the others' behavior so as to be able to interact successfully with them. If I take the 'others' to be human agents, I assume that they are engaged in a similar 'reflective' process of (a) trying to make sense of my action by attributing to me views about reasons and motives which are compatible with my behavior and which they find comprehensible, and (b) reevaluating their own views in the light of their experience with me.[74]

This reflective process of interpretation is an integral part of human interaction; it is the only possible context for the confirmation of a critical theory. The epistemic principles the agents use won't in general be something they have clearly formulated, and many of their normative beliefs, views about freedom and coercion etc. will be merely tacit.

---

[73] Cf. Quine (1969), pp. 1ff.
[74] TG 190ff.

Their epistemic principles aren't just out there to be observed and described; in formulating them the critical theory is in part 'constructing' them. Formulating them may impose on them a determinateness they did not before possess, and may cause the agents to change other parts. When I describe the epistemic principles of the 'addressed' agents from which the critical argument begins, this description itself is proleptic; the epistemic principles are 'theirs' in the sense that they can be brought to recognize these principles as a good rational reconstruction of conceptions underlying their behavior. But, of course, the basic assumption of the critical theory is that simply bringing certain attitudes, beliefs, behavior patterns etc. to full consciousness changes them. This assumption seems quite reasonable in many cases. It is also true that proponents of the critical theory think that through the complex process of coming to adopt the critical theory certain beliefs, attitudes, etc. are not just changed, but *refuted,* shown to be false. With that we are back to the question of the cognitive standing of the critical theory and of the attitudes and beliefs it treats.

All the members of the Frankfurt School are agreed that the critical theory must be knowledge and must show ideological beliefs and attitudes to be false. Otherwise the critical theory couldn't have its proper emancipatory effect, which depends on its ability to make those who adopt it able to withstand the pressure of the legitimatory apparatus of society. Critical theories must be 'true' because the legitimizing ideologies of the society claim to be 'true.'

The positivists would have said that neither legitimizing world-pictures nor critical theories can be true *or* false. Perhaps they were wrong only to draw from this the conclusion that world-pictures and critical theories are therefore meaningless and that there is no way rationally to decide between them, that any choice is a *mere* preference. Why accept the alternative: Science *or* mere, brute preference?

Agents can act in ways that are more or less enlightened; the freedom of communication and discussion they enjoy and their freedom to form and acquire beliefs and preferences is a matter of degree; agents can be more or less reflective. To what extent a critical theory is enlightening and emancipatory may then equally be a matter of degree. If rational argumentation can lead to the conclusion that a critical theory represents the most advanced position of consciousness available to us in our given historical situation, why the obsession with whether or not we may call it 'true?'

This is not a form of the relativism the members of the Frankfurt School rightly reject. If it is closer to Adorno's historicism than to Habermas' recent views about the 'ideal speech situation,' that seems to me to be an advantage: the critical theory is better off without the transcendental baggage.

If a critical theory is not a true 'scientific' theory, not a part of empirical social *science* strictly so called, we might think of it as part of the wider enterprise of social theory or social philosophy. Not all empirical social inquiry must have the structure of critical theory, but the construction of an empirically informed critical theory of society might be a legitimate and rational human aspiration.

WORKS CITED

Apel, Karl-Otto et al., *Hermeneutik und Ideologiekritik*, Frankfurt: Suhrkamp, 1971.

Barry, Brian, *Sociologists, Economists, and Democracy*, Chicago: University of Chicago Press, 1978.

Barth, Hans, *Wahrheit und Ideologie*, Frankfurt: Suhrkamp, 1975.

Brodbeck, May, *Readings in Philosophy of Social Science*, New York: Macmillan, 1968.

Burkert, Walter, *Structure and History in Greek Mythology and Ritual*, Berkeley and Los Angeles: University of California Press, 1979.

Carr, E. H., *What is History?*, New York: Knopf, 1962.

Cohen, G. A., *Karl Marx's Theory of History: A Defense*, Princeton: Princeton University Press, 1978.

Dumont, Louis, *Homo Hierarchicus*, Chicago: University of Chicago Press, 1970.

Frankfurt, Harry, 'Freedom of the Will and the Concept of a Person,' *Journal of Philosophy*, 68, 1971.

Freud, Sigmund, *Die Zukunft einer Illusion*, cited from vol. IX, *Freud-Studienausgabe*, Frankfurt: Fischer, 1974.

Friedrich, C. J. and Brzezinski, Z., *Totalitarian Dictatorship and Autocracy*, Cambridge, Mass.: Harvard University Press, 1956.

Geertz, Clifford, *Islam Observed*, Chicago: University of Chicago Press, 1971.

Harris, Marvin, *Cows, Pigs, Wars, and Witches: The Riddle of Culture*, New York: Random House, 1974.

Hirschman, Albert, *The Passions and the Interests: Political Arguments for Capitalism before its Triumph*, Princeton: Princeton University Press, 1977.

Jay, Martin, *The Dialectical Imagination*, Boston: Little, Brown and Co., 1973.

Kaplan, David and Manners, Robert, *Culture Theory*, Englewood Cliffs, NJ: Prentice-Hall, 1972.

Kortian, Garbis, *Métacritique*, Cambridge: Cambridge University Press, 1980.

Kroeber, Alfred and Kluckhohn, Clyde. 'Culture: A Critical Review of Concepts and Definitions,' Papers of the Peabody Museum of American Archaeology and Ethnology, vol. 47, Cambridge, Mass. 1952.

Laing, R. D. and Esterson, A., *Sanity, Madness and the Family*, London Tavistock Publications, 1964.

Larrain, Jorge, *The Concept of Ideology*, Athens, Georgia: The University of Georgia Press, 1979.

Lenin, V. I. *What is to be Done?* in *The Lenin Anthology*, ed. R. Tucker, New York: Norton, 1975.

Lichtheim, George, *The Concept of Ideology*, New York: Random House, 1967.

Luhmann, Niklas, *Soziologische Aufklärung*, Köln und Opladen, 1970.

Lukács, Georg, *Geschichte und Klassenbewußtsein,* Neuwied und Berlin: Luchter-hand, 1968.

McMurtry, John, *The Structure of Marx's World-View,* Princeton: Princeton University Press, 1978.

Mannheim, Karl, *Ideology and Utopia,* New York: Harcourt, Brace, and World, 1936.

Marcuse, Herbert, *Eros and Civilization,* Boston: Beacon, 1955.

Marx, Karl and Engels, Friedrich, *Werke,* Berlin: Dietz Verlag, 1956–

Merton, Robert, *Social Theory and Social Structure,* Glencoe: The Free Press, 1957.

Nietzsche, Friedrich, *Zur Geneologie der Moral. Werke,* Band III (herausgegeben von Karl Schlechta), Frankfurt: Ullstein, 1969.

O'Neill, John. *On Critical Theory,* New York: Seabury, 1976.

Plamenatz, John, *Ideology,* London, 1970.

Popper, Karl, *The Poverty of Historicism,* New York: Harper & Row, 1964.

Popper, Karl, *The Open Society and its Enemies,* Princeton: Princeton University Press, 1971.

Quine, W. V. O., *From a Logical Point of View,* New York: Harper, 1963.

Quine, W. V. O., *Ontological Relativity and Other Essays,* New York: Columbia, 1969.

Runciman, W. G., *Sociology in its Place,* Cambridge: Cambridge University Press, 1970.

Sahlins, Marshall, *Culture and Practical Reason,* Chicago: University of Chicago Press, 1976.

Sahlins, Marshall, *Tribesmen,* Englewood Cliffs, NJ: Prentice-Hall, 1968.

Seliger, Martin, *The Marxian Conception of Ideology,* Cambridge: Cambridge University Press, 1977.

Service, Elman, *The Hunters,* Englewood Cliffs, NJ: Prentice-Hall, 1966.

Theunissen, Michael, *Gesellschaft und Geschichte: Zur Kritik der kritischen Theorie,* Berlin: de Gruyter, 1969.

Tucker, R. (ed.), *Marx–Engels Reader,* New York: Norton, 1971.

Turnbull, Colin, *The Mountain People,* New York: Simon and Schuster, 1972.

Waxman, Chaim (ed.), *The End of Ideology Debate,* New York: Simon & Schuster, 1968.

INDEX

action, political, 74f, 84f, 86
Adorno, T. W., 1, 3, 33n, 63, 64, 81, 94
anticipate, 57, 66
assent, free, 78ff, 84ff, 89ff
  universal, 86f, 89
Augustine, 25

Barry, B., 9n
Barth, H., 4n
Bell, D., 11
Benjamin, W., 22n, 57
Bergmann, G., 14n
Brodbeck, M., 14n
Burkert, W., 6n

Chomsky, N., 67
coercion, 2, 50, 55, 58, 60–70 passim, 72–6,
  78ff, 90f
  self-imposed, 2, 58–61, 70, 73ff
  see also freedom; Herrschaft; repression;
  frustration; compulsion; unfree existence
Cohen, G., 9n, 18n
compulsion, of the better argument, 72, 75
  to believe, 75, 86n
confirmation, see critical theory, confirmation.
consciousness, form of, 12f
  false, see ideology; delusion, ideological
consensus, 72, 88f
  rational, 30
consensus theory of truth, 66f
contextualism, 63ff
critical theory
  addressed to particular agents, 63, 69, 74,
  76, 78f, 81, 84, 86f
  as self-consciousness of process of emancipation, 58, 76, 85, 87
  confirmation of, 1f, 55, 75ff, 85, 88ff
  effects of, see emancipation; enlightenment
  embedded in cultural context, 90
  required for emancipation, 76, 85, 92
criticism
  along the epistemic dimension, 21f,
  26–31, 69f
  along the functional dimension, 21f, 31–6,
  69f

along the genetic dimension, 21f, 36–44,
  69f
  internal, 33, 64f, 78, 87f
  see also ideology; reflective unacceptability; falsity, ideological
culture, 4ff, 22
cultural context, see critical theory
cultural tradition as source of ideals, 63, 82f,
  88

delusion, ideological, 12, 19, 20f, 52, 60f, 65,
  75, 82–4, 87
  distinguished by Freud from error and
  illusion, 39ff
  never complete, 87f
Dewey, J., 36
dialectics, 22, 33n, 36
Dumont, L., 69n

emancipation, 2, 55, 58–61, 70, 82ff
  full emancipation distinct from
  enlightenment, 73–5, 86
  possible without enlightenment, 84
  criteria for success, 85–91
  see also enlightenment; freedom
Engels, F., 19
enlightenment, 2, 45, 52, 83
  see also emancipation; freedom
epistemic principles, 61–5, 68, 79f, 92ff
equality, 65, 69f
  see also inequality

falsity, ideological, 12, 19, 20f, 32ff, 38ff,
  60ff, 69
  in virtue of epistemic properties, 13–15,
  26–31, 32n, 38f, 69f
  in virtue of functional properties, 13,
  15–19, 36, 69f
  in virtue of genetic properties, 13, 19–22,
  32n, 36–44, 69f
  see also delusion, ideological; criticism
freedom
  agents' views of, 64, 78ff
  as final state of process of emancipation,
  76
  conditions of, 53f, 60, 72, 78, 89
  of discussion, 62, 65ff, 73
  from delusion, 12, 60

freedom (*cont.*)
  see also emancipation; coercion; assent,
    free
Freud, S., 1, 39, 40, 41f
Friedrich, C. and Brzezinski, Z., 11n
frustration
  of attempts to realize the 'good life,' 63
  of given desires, 16–19, 32, 34ff, 59, 65,
    73, 75, 76, 85ff
  changes in level of, 74f, 85f, 91
  experience of, as motivation of critical
    theory, 80ff, 86
  of which agents are not fully aware, 81ff,
    87, 90
  see also coercion; freedom

Gadamer, H.-G., 55n
Geertz, C., 9n
Giegel, H., 74n
good life, conception of the, 48, 63, 68, 82,
  88

Harris, M., 48n
Hegel, G. W. F., 33n
hermeneutics, 55n, 85, 92ff
Herrschaft, 15ff, 31ff, 69
surplus, 17f, 35f, 69
Hirschman, A., 46n, 48n
historicism, 34, 63, 94
Horkheimer, M., 1, 3

ideal speech situation, 65–70, 72f, 85f
Ideologiekritik, *see* criticism; ideology; delusion, ideological
ideology
  accepted for reasons agents could not
    acknowledge, 20f, 29f, 43f
  as artificially restricted form of conscious-
    ness, 83f, 87
  as seemingly autonomous form of con-
    sciousness in fact bound to particular
    interests, 74
  as expression of class-position, 19f, 37ff
  as socially necessary illusion, 15f
  in descriptive sense, 5–12
  in pejorative sense, 12–22, 26–44, 87
  in positive sense, 22–6, 38, 51, 87
  in programmatic sense, 11f
  in purely descriptive sense, 5ff
  in the sense of 'world-view,' 9ff, 15, 22,
    31ff, 50f
  see also delusion, ideological; falsity,
    ideological; criticism
illusion, *see* delusion
illusion, objective, 61, 70ff
  see also delusion; falsity, ideological;
    objectification mistake
inequality, 16ff, 73f, 86f
  see also equality; repression
interests, 23ff, 34f, 46ff, 58, 59n
  as explanation of error, 41f
  class, 37f, 84f
  conflicting, 73f

general, 14, 27, 38
particular, 14, 27, 38, 74
phenomenal, 45, 48
real, true, objective, 2f, 12, 45, 66, 73, 75,
  76f, 86f; perfect knowledge approach
  to, 48–54; optimal conditions approach
  to, 48–54; action contrary to, 12
universalizable, 68

Jay, M., 3n

Kaplan, D. and Manners, R., 4n, 5n
Kortian, G., 3n
Kroeber, A. and Kluckhohn, C., 4n

Laing, R. and Esterson, A., 74n
Larrain, J., 4n, 18n
legitimation, 15ff, 31ff, 59f, 62, 67ff, 71f,
  74f, 81, 83, 84
Lenin, V., 23
Lichtheim, G., 4n
Luhmann, N., 21n
Lukács, G., 24, 37, 84

McMurtry, J., 9n
Mannheim, K., 7n, 11n, 19, 20n, 37n, 39n
Marcuse, H., 1, 3, 17n, 98n, 37, 81, 88
Marx, K., 1ff, 9n, 14n, 18n
Marxism, 1, 5, 17, 36f, 51n, 56f, 71, 76f
Merleau-Ponty, M., 23n
Merton, R., 14
motives, motivation, 19ff, 29ff, 39–44, 54,
  92f

necessary, historically, 17, 19, 35f
necessity, theoretical vs. practical, 77
needs
  distinguished from wants, desires, etc.,
    46–8
  existential, 22, 25, 40
  false, 36, 88
  social interpretation of, 35f
Nietzsche, F., 43f

objectification mistake, 14, 15n, 27, 29n, 71f
objectify, *see* theory, objectifying
objective illusion, *see* illusion, objective
objective interest, *see* interest, real
objective power, 58, 60f, 70, 73f
objectivity, 71ff
opiate, 84, 87

Peirce, C., 36
Pilot, H., 64n
Plamenatz, J., 6, 9n
Popper, K., 11n
positivism, 2, 13f, 26–31, 94
psychoanalysis, 1f, 19f, 39, 51n, 74, 86n, 90n

Quine, W., 10, 89n, 93n

rationality, 26–31, 57f, 66, 69, 87, 88
reflection, 2, 56, 63ff, 91, 93; *see also*
  self-reflection; theory, reflective

reflective acceptability, 61ff, 68ff, 76, 91
repression
    normative, 16ff, 34f
    surplus, 17f, 35f, 69
Runciman, W., 19

Sahlins, M., 5n, 35n
scientism, 27, 77
self-fulfilling beliefs, 14f, 27
self-knowledge, 49, 51, 53f, 63f
self-reflection, 61, 70ff
Seliger, M., 23n
Service, E., 5n

theory
    objectifying, 2, 55, 79f, 91f
Theunissen, M., 3n

transcendentalism, 64ff, 94f
Turnbull, C., 49n, 50

unconscious determinants of behavior, 61,
    70, 74f
unfree existence, 58, 60, 75
utopia, 54
utopianism, 53, 76f
utopian kernel, content, 82, 88

wants, desires, preferences, 22ff, 35f, 45ff
    false, 36
    unconscious, 81ff
    what agents could want, 83f
Wellmer, A., 1, 12n, 13n, 18n, 33n, 48n, 77n,
    78n, 80n, 82n, 88n
wishful thinking, 41ff
Wissenschaft, 88ff
world-view, world-picture, see ideology, as
    world-view